KEEP CALM:
102 Pieces of Wisdom to Find Peace, Stop Overthinking, and Carry On With Your Life

by Nick Trenton

www.NickTrenton.com

Table of Contents

Chapter 1: The Power of Considering Alternative Explanations 9

Chapter 2: Sometimes You Shouldn't Keep "Looking Within" 13

Chapter 3: Action Matters 17

Chapter 4: What Are You Really Afraid Of? 21

Chapter 5: How to Say YES, How to Say NO 25

Chapter: 6: Your Inner Voice Helps You Self-Regulate 29

Chapter 7: Feeling Depressed? Be Kind 33

Chapter 8: The Good News in Bad News 37

Chapter 9: Mindful Movement Lowers Stress 43

Chapter 10: Bothered by Negative, Unwanted Thoughts? Just Throw Them Away 47

Chapter 11: Take that Leap—Do Something! 51

Chapter 12: The Wisdom of "So What?" 55

Chapter 13: The Past Is Gone 59

Chapter 14: Drop the Blame 63

Chapter 15: Needs Versus Wants 67

Chapter 16: Cultivating Emotional Discernment 71

Chapter 17: Remember, YOU'RE the Master 75

Chapter 18: Feel the Fear and Do It Anyway 79

Chapter 19: It All Happens Here, in the Present 83

Chapter 20: Just Breathe 89

Chapter 21: Worry . . . But Do It on Your Terms 93

Chapter 22: Find Relief in Ritual 97

Chapter 23: Two Stressed People Means Less Stress 101

Chapter 24: "And What Does that Mean . . .?" 105

Chapter 25: You Need to Unplug 109

Chapter 26: Stick to the Facts 113

Chapter 27: The Fastest Way to Find Perspective 119

Chapter 28: What's Your Default State? 123

Chapter 29: Don't Sweat the Small Stuff 127

Chapter 30: Getting Comfy with the Gray Areas 131

Chapter 31: You Don't Have to be a Hero 137

Chapter 32: Understanding Your Zone of Control 143

Chapter 33: Don't Suffer More than You Have To 149

Chapter 34: Worry Has No Function 153

Chapter 35: Pet Your Stress Away 157

Chapter 36: Plan in Reverse 161

Chapter 37: Put It in Black and White 165

Chapter 38: Put a Label on It 169

Chapter 39: Count Your Blessings 173

Chapter 40: The You Behind the Thoughts 177

Chapter 41: It's All Interpretation 181

Chapter 42: The Value of Letting Go 183

Chapter 43: Ride It Out 187

Chapter 44: Stop Comparing Yourself 191

Chapter 45: You Can Tell a Different Story 195

Chapter 46: How Are Your Perceptions Serving You? 199

Chapter 47: Enough Is Really Enough 203

Chapter 48: Resilience Comes from Purpose 207

Chapter 49: Make Friends with Your Demons 211

Chapter 50: Have a Growth Mindset 215

Chapter 51: Avoid Choice Paralysis 219

Chapter 1: The Power of Considering Alternative Explanations

"Most misunderstandings in the world could be avoided if people would simply take the time to ask, "What else could this mean?" —Shannon L. Alder

In the hustle and bustle of our daily lives, it's all too easy to fall into the trap of quick judgments and assumptions. Misunderstandings abound, and they often stem from a lack of willingness to explore alternative perspectives and intentional pauses. Shannon L. Alder's wise words urge us to pause and ask ourselves, "What else could this mean?"

Most of us are good at asking "What could this mean?" but we stumble when we latch on to the first or only answer to the question. By simply asking what else an event could mean, we can unlock a world of possibilities and maintain a balanced perspective even in the face of negative events and create a healthy space between our experiences and reactions. In that space we can grow, fix problems, create, or become the better version of ourselves we know we can be.

Ask "What Else Could This Mean?"

When faced with a negative event or an ambiguous situation, our default response is often to latch on to the most convenient or self-serving explanation. And the most convenient explanation, by the way, isn't necessarily one that

- Helps us,
- Accurately reflects the world, or
- Makes us feel good.

It's just the one that fits the frame of mind we're already occupying. If your frame of mind is blind panic and terror when someone points a knife at you, you'll probably decide it means they want to kill you. But it's only when you ask, "What *else* could it mean?" that you are able to see that they're just offering you a tool to help you cut the carrots for the soup you're both making.

Let's consider a more everyday scenario: A close friend cancels plans at the last minute. What does it mean? If you're in a particular mindset, it's proof that nobody loves you. But instead of jumping to conclusions and assuming they no longer value your friendship, we could entertain the possibility that they might be facing unexpected personal challenges or simply need some time for self-care. They could have an emergency on their hands or be ill. Who knows, they could be making soup!

In moments of criticism or rejection, it's easy to internalize these experiences as reflections of our worth. Yet, by practicing the habit of considering alternative explanations, we can protect ourselves from blindly believing the worst possible interpretations. Maybe you're a total failure and about to get fired any minute now . . . or maybe your boss has a point and him pointing out that you were late that morning doesn't mean you're a bad human being.

By incorporating the question "What else could this mean?" into our daily lives, we nurture a habit of seeking multiple perspectives. This habit helps us transcend our initial reactions, fostering a more balanced and empathetic understanding of negative events. In turn, we can approach life with a greater sense of presence and embrace the possibilities that lie beyond our immediate interpretations.

Slowing Down for Mindful Living

In our fast-paced world, where instant reactions and impulsive decisions often take the forefront, it is crucial to cultivate the skill of slowing down the processing time between experiencing something and reacting to it.

Basically, you can't ask, "What else does this mean?"—or anything else, for that matter—if you don't give yourself a few moments to do so before reacting. By extending this space, we create room for mindfulness and intentional living, ultimately allowing us to be more present, less anxious, and less prone to overthinking.

Think of a passing comment that triggers a negative emotional response. Instead of immediately lashing out or retreating into a shell of defensiveness, we can choose to slow down.

In moments of stress or pressure, our natural inclination is often to react swiftly, driven by our fight-or-flight instincts. Emotion is lightning quick and automatic; careful consideration takes a little longer. By intentionally slowing down the processing time, we gain the power to respond thoughtfully rather than impulsively.

For example, imagine receiving an urgent work email that triggers feelings of overwhelm and anxiety. Instead of immediately plunging into a frenzy of frantic multitasking, we can take a few mindful breaths and ask ourselves, "What else could this mean?" This pause allows us to breathe before making deliberate choices that align with our values and well-being.

Slowing down the processing time is particularly crucial in our digital age, where information bombards us incessantly. When encountering news or social media posts that evoke strong emotions, instead of instantly reacting or sharing our immediate thoughts, we can practice a mindful pause. Slowing down the processing time in the face of provocative content helps us avoid unnecessary conflict and be in the present moment.

A big surprise when trying out this practice is that some things *don't actually mean anything*. In other words, a trigger can float by and grab our attention, but that doesn't mean we have to react, and it certainly doesn't mean we have to react in a pre-destined way. We don't have to accept it *or* push against it—we can simply choose to detach and place our attention elsewhere.

In our personal relationships, the practice of slowing down our processing time is an invaluable tool for reducing misunderstandings. Imagine how many interpersonal arguments you could defuse by simply pausing and choosing not to react. Imagine how many stressful rabbit holes, tangents, and unnecessary trains of thought you could avoid if you merely pause long enough to say, "Wait, do I even want to go there?"

Chapter 2: Sometimes You Shouldn't Keep "Looking Within"

"A person who thinks all the time has nothing to think about except thoughts. So, he loses touch with reality and lives in a world of illusions." —Alan Watts

Digital buzz and constant chatter—our world is awash with perpetual distractions, a cacophony of beeps and notifications. It's a place where the art of self-reflection often becomes a refuge—a sanctuary to which we retreat, seeking solace amidst the relentless noise. As the renowned philosopher Alan Watts astutely observed, an unbridled fixation on introspection can lead us astray, causing us to lose touch with reality and plunge headlong into a world of illusions. Striking the delicate equilibrium between delving into our inner selves and engaging with the external world is the cornerstone of a life marked by presence, reduced anxiety, and liberation from overthinking.

Balancing Introspection and External Experiences

While introspection holds the key to understanding our motivations, fears, and dreams, an excess of it can pull us out of reality's embrace. Just like a pendulum, swinging too far toward constant self-analysis can lead to a life spent outside the vibrant tapestry of the present moment. We become ensnared in our thoughts, trapped in a maze of our own making. It's a paradox: The more we dwell on our thoughts, the more detached we become from the very experiences that give rise to those thoughts.

Imagine a child tells his dad he is afraid of a monster under their bed. The dad, trying his best, sits down and addresses the problem. He makes a compelling rational argument for why there couldn't logically be a monster, and even if there was, there are a dozen contingency plans for what they'd do to manage it. The dad goes on to explain the boy's deepest unconscious psychological fears and how the monster is just an abstract symbol of the unknown. The boy and his dad talk long into the night, for hours, about the philosophical and metaphysical ramifications of the monster myth, and what it represents both politically and culturally, and how they are going to rewrite that fear narrative, reclaim the word "monster," and release blocked psychic and libidinal energy and channel it into the tasks of mastery that reflect the child's developmental crises.

The child is still afraid of what's under the bed, though.

The next day, his mom impatiently tells the boy to just look under the bed himself.

"Is there a monster there?"

"I guess not."

Thinking helps us solve problems.

Overthinking *is* a problem.

Consider a scenario where you've spent hours dissecting a conversation you had with a colleague. You've parsed every word, every nuance, to the point where the actual moment has blurred into a haze of overthinking. Meanwhile, your colleague has moved on, engrossed in new conversations and experiences. The excessive introspection, while well-intentioned, has distanced you from the tangible world—from the laughter echoing in the hallway, the aroma of coffee wafting from the break room, the real connections being forged in the present.

Similarly, imagine a traveler who meticulously plans every detail of their journey before even setting foot on the path. They've studied the maps, read reviews, and crafted an intricate itinerary. Yet, when they finally embark, the world surprises them with unforeseen vistas, unexpected detours, and the magic of spontaneous encounters. The traveler who lives solely in their plans misses out on the essence of travel itself—the act of surrendering to the unknown, letting go of rigid expectations, and embracing the beauty of unscripted moments.

In the pursuit of balance, we must weave introspection into the fabric of our lives without allowing it to unravel the threads of reality. We can cultivate mindfulness by engaging our senses in the present—feeling the earth beneath our feet, savoring the flavors of a meal, and truly listening to the stories of others. This reconnection with the tangible world invites us to be active participants in the narrative of life, rather than mere spectators lost in the labyrinth of our thoughts.

Defending Against Negative Self-Deception

In our journey toward self-improvement and mindful living, we often tread the delicate line between self-reflection and self-deception.

The human mind is a master of constructing narratives, especially ones that serve to shield us from discomfort or accountability. We can easily slip into a state of negative self-deception—a mental terrain where we justify our inaction, rationalize our shortcomings, and create elaborate stories to avoid confronting our own limitations. It's a refuge that feels safe but ultimately robs us of the chance to confront our fears and grow from them. We may convince ourselves that we're doing something or solving problems, all while we are really doing nothing.

Imagine someone striving to launch their own business. They spend months perfecting their product, crafting marketing strategies, and building an online presence. Yet, as launch day approaches, a nagging self-doubt creeps in. Instead of facing this uncertainty head-on, they distract themselves with busy work, convince themselves that the timing isn't right, and meticulously plan every detail to evade the risk of failure. While it may seem like they're being meticulous, they're actually trapped in a web of self-deception—an illusion that shields them from the vulnerability of facing potential setbacks.

How do you get real with yourself?

Honest conversations with mentors, friends, or peers can offer valuable perspectives that cut through the haze of self-deception. Seeking out constructive criticism and opening ourselves up to vulnerability enables us to see our blind spots and challenge the illusions we create. It's a humbling process that requires embracing discomfort. Sometimes, however, we need to just look under the bed!

Chapter 3: Action Matters

"Because we feel vulnerable about the future, we keep trying to solve problems in our head." —David Carbonell

As David Carbonell insightfully notes, our discomfort with the unknown often leads us down a path of incessant problem-solving within the confines of our minds. Except it's not real problem-solving at all. We grapple with hypothetical scenarios, concoct intricate plans, and endlessly attempt to predict the unpredictable. But what if instead of this fruitless endeavor, we could find a way to be comfortable with vulnerability and embrace the uncontrollable nature of the future?

Embracing Vulnerability and Uncertainty

Imagine releasing the tight grip of control you've exerted over every possible outcome. Visualize that moment when you take a deep breath, loosen your grip on the steering wheel, and allow the winds of uncertainty to guide your course. It's a shift that requires not blind surrender, but rather a deep trust in your innate ability to adapt and navigate whatever challenges come your way.

Think back to a time when life veered unexpectedly off-course. Perhaps it was a sudden job loss or a surprise opportunity that turned your carefully planned trajectory on its head. Remember how, despite the initial shock, you managed to recalibrate your direction and forge ahead? In those moments, you tapped into an unexplored reservoir of resilience and creativity. By relinquishing control, you opened yourself to unforeseen possibilities, finding solutions you might never have imagined had you clung to the illusion of total mastery.

Remember our overthinking backpacker? While meticulous planning is essential, there comes a point when the trail is no longer predetermined, and each step brings new challenges. By learning to adapt to changing weather, unexpected detours, and the occasional wrong turn, the backpacker develops a heightened sense of resourcefulness. It's this cultivated ability to thrive amidst the uncertainty that not only defines the essence of the journey but also holds the potential to transform the traveler's perspective on life itself.

To be comfortable with vulnerability and uncertainty doesn't mean forfeiting responsibility or direction. It's a matter of acknowledging that no amount of preconceived planning can predict every twist and turn ahead. As you stand at the intersection of anticipation and the unknown, remind yourself that it's your capacity to flex, pivot, and adapt that truly defines your journey.

From Thought to Action

Sometimes, our brain gets caught up in "What if?" and traps itself in endless brainstorming. As we contemplate potential scenarios, our mind's landscape becomes . . . cluttered.

"What if I ask her out and she says no?"

"What if she laughs in my face?"

"What if she already has a boyfriend?"

"What if I offend her?"

"What if I embarrass myself?"

All the above questions are useless. That's because all they can do is invite conjecture and guesswork. There is one surefire way to figure out what will happen—you talk to her. You could spend a week ruminating over the endless (awful) possibilities, or you could take single action, note what happens, and move on in the space of five minutes.

We're talking about an important mindset shift—a transition from contemplation to action.

Another example: the entrepreneur striving to launch a startup. While careful planning and market analysis are essential, the ultimate success lies not in endless theoretical discussions but in launching a prototype, gathering feedback, and refining the product iteratively. The entrepreneur learns to replace the cycle of "what ifs" with a steady stream of "what's next."

Let's take another instance, that of a writer grappling with the challenge of starting a novel. Overwhelmed by the vast expanse of blank pages and the prospect of critique, the writer easily finds refuge in elaborate planning and character development. Yet, the true breakthrough comes when the writer sets aside the mental blueprint and begins to type the opening words. It's a leap of faith, an act of honoring the present moment, and a tangible step toward the desired future outcome.

The key to escaping the trap of overthinking and uncertainty lies in fostering a bias toward action. Even action that is imperfect. Even action taken when you're a little unsure and a little scared.

Start small, with one manageable step, and then another. Instead of fixating on potential pitfalls, focus on the progress you make, however modest it may seem. Remember, the future outcome you desire isn't achieved through thought alone—it's forged through the fires of action.

Chapter 4: What Are You Really Afraid Of?

"Man is not worried by real problems so much as by his imagined anxieties about real problems."— Epictetus

Picture this: a serene lake surrounded by lush greenery, reflecting the clear blue sky above. You sit by the water's edge, basking in the tranquility of the moment. Yet, amidst this peaceful scene, your mind starts to wander. Suddenly, you're engulfed by thoughts of potential job loss, strained relationships, and uncertain futures. These are what Epictetus calls "imagined anxieties." You are in heaven, but your mind makes you think you are in hell.

Questioning Unbounded Fears

Fear has a function. Your ancestors used it to help identify and flee from genuine threats to their survival—for example, the quintessential saber-toothed beast rustling in the grass. Your body doesn't know the difference between a thing and a *thought about* a thing, however. Fast forward to modern-day life. You could be sitting quietly in an armchair, and when you read about a fictional saber-toothed beast, you experience the exact same physiological reaction as your ancient ancestors did—except it's not real. Modern man's ability to think and imagine, then, is also an ability to terrify himself for no good reason.

Take, for instance, the job interview you're anticipating next week. Your mind concocts a narrative of stumbling over your words, being rejected, and facing a bleak future. Yet, in reality, the interview is still in the future, and your current anxiety serves only to cloud your present moments. Or consider the social event you're dreading—you fear awkward conversations and judgment. But aren't you projecting yourself into a future that may not align with what truly transpires?

By questioning the basis of these imagined anxieties, we can unravel their grip on us. Ask yourself: What evidence do I have that this feared outcome will happen? Is there another, more balanced perspective I could adopt? A big question is: am I reacting to this situation, or my thoughts about this situation? Asking this means you're free to wonder if there may be a more useful way to think about things.

Embracing Present Action

Sometimes, we also find ourselves entangled in the rhythm of anticipation, yearning for a future that sparkles with our dreams. Yet, in our fervent fixation on the horizon, we risk missing the enchantment of the steps we take today. Epictetus's words hold a mirror to our restless minds, revealing that our true struggles lie not in the tangible challenges that confront us but in the mirage of anxieties we weave around them.

Imagine the aspiring writer who dreams of penning a bestseller. Every keystroke carries the weight of imagined expectations—reviews, accolades, and the shimmering allure of fame. In this future-focused trance, the writer overlooks the beauty of each word crafted, the stories woven, and the lessons learned in the process. They also overlook how boring the writing process can be on some days, and so, when their writing journey is less than exceptional, they lose motivation and quit.

Epictetus's wisdom echoes here, urging us to draw our gaze away from the alluring horizon and anchor it firmly in the nurturing soil of the present moment. By pouring our passion into each chapter and savoring the creative journey, we nurture not only our craft but also the fulfillment that comes from simply doing our best. We embed ourselves in the only place we can actually take action: the present.

The same holds true in the sphere of personal growth. We yearn to transform, to become the best versions of ourselves. But this very focus could have us failing to engage meaningfully with our imperfect, present selves, and all the hard work we have to put into life in the here and now.

Usually, when we ruminate, our minds are in the past or in the future, worried about what has already happened or stewing over what might happen—but hasn't actually happened and may never happen. Both of these positions are inherently disempowering. Anxiety that is projected into the past or future can grow unchecked to any size and take on any outlandish shape. It's only when we pull our thoughts back to the present moment that our problem becomes smaller, more realistic, and actionable.

Take a look at the following thoughts:

A: I've gone for five interviews so far and never gotten the job. I'm never going to get one. I'm doomed. Everything is stacked against me, and I'm such a loser. How am I going to get out of this mess?

B: I can't change yesterday. Things are challenging, but I have some resources available to me, and I'm doing my best. I found a job before, and I'll figure out a way to find one again. Now, what can I do today, right now, to make that easier? I know it's scary, but I just have to identify the next step.

Which thought makes you feel better? Which feels not only kinder but more realistic? Perhaps most importantly, which thought is likely to inspire meaningful, practical action that will genuinely help solve your problem?

Chapter 5: How to Say YES, How to Say NO

"You have to decide what your highest priorities are and have the courage pleasantly, smilingly, and non-apologetically—to say "no" to other things. And the way to do that is by having a bigger yes burning inside."—Stephen Covey

In the modern whirlwind of obligations, opportunities, and distractions, it's easy to lose sight of what truly matters. In these moments, Stephen Covey's wisdom is a guiding beacon in the sea of daily demands. How do we harness the power of this approach to create a life that aligns with our deepest desires?

Defining Your "Bigger Yes"

Defining your "bigger yes" is akin to setting your life's mission statement. It's about pinpointing the overarching goal that sparks your passion and excitement. This "bigger yes" is your compass, directing your energy toward endeavors that resonate with your values.

Imagine you've been invited to join a new project at work, but you're already juggling multiple commitments. By defining your "bigger yes"—perhaps it's advancing in your career while maintaining a healthy work-life balance—you'll be able to evaluate whether this new opportunity propels you closer to or further from your desired destination.

Without a clear vision, anxiety often finds a way to creep into our lives. We're haunted by doubts and second-guessing, constantly questioning if we're on the right path. But with a "bigger yes" in hand, those doubts have less of an impact on us. When deciding whether to commit to a social event or prioritize self-care, your "bigger yes" becomes the litmus test. Does this align with your greater purpose? Does it resonate with your priorities?

Many of us feel uncomfortable saying "no" because, well, it sounds negative. We worry we're letting people down, missing out on opportunities, or being rigid or unreasonable. But when your decisions are guided by your "bigger yes," the anxiety of uncertainty loses its grip. You think of it not as saying "no" to A but saying "yes" to B. Each of us is human, and we only have finite resources, time, and energy. We cannot do everything. That means if we value some things, we *have to* place other things in second place.

Take Jane, for example, a marketing professional with aspirations of launching her own consultancy. She defines her "bigger yes" as being an independent entrepreneur who empowers small businesses through strategic branding. When she's presented with the opportunity to lead a massive corporate campaign, she evaluates it against her vision. The lucrative offer might tempt her, but her "bigger yes" whispers that her heart belongs to fostering local entrepreneurship. With this clarity, she confidently declines the offer, knowing it takes her a step closer to her desired destination.

In a world abundant with choices, knowing your "bigger yes" streamlines decision-making. It's the art of saying "no" without guilt or hesitation, because every "no" is an affirmation of your commitment to your purpose. As you nurture your sense of purpose and prioritize the pursuits that fuel your passions, you create a shield against the chaos of overcommitment and the anxiety of aimlessness. Your "bigger yes" is your personal creed, and with it, you're on your way to a life rich in meaning and fulfillment.

Mastering the "Positive No"

In the pursuit of being present and living with intention, the journey toward a more balanced life inevitably also involves mastering the art of saying "no" graciously but firmly—the positive no. As you navigate the delicate dance between nurturing relationships and safeguarding your time and energy, remember that a positive no is not just about asserting your boundaries; it's about deepening your connections.

Imagine you've been invited to yet another social event during a week already brimming with commitments. Instead of feeling anxious about juggling your schedule or agonizing over how to decline, practice the positive no. Begin by acknowledging the invitation warmly, expressing gratitude for being included. Empathize with the host's efforts in organizing the event, and then firmly communicate your decision to decline, explaining that your current schedule doesn't allow for additional commitments at this time. However, offer an alternative—perhaps you can't attend the event, but you'd be thrilled to catch up over coffee next week (if, in fact, you truthfully would be thrilled! There's no point dodging overcommitment today only to set up a bigger one for yourself tomorrow).

Boundaries are the invisible guardians of your well-being, ensuring that you have the capacity to show up fully in every facet of your life. They are not about other people or what they choose to do or not do—they're about *you* and your limits, goals, and desires. That's why a good boundary doesn't convince, explain, justify, or manipulate anyone. It isn't an apology or a request for permission. It is merely an assertion of who you are and what you value.

As you practice the art of the positive no, remember that each interaction is a chance to deepen your relationships and enhance your presence. It's an opportunity to communicate not just what you're declining, but also what you're affirming—your commitment to your priorities, your respect for others' needs, and your dedication to fostering meaningful connections.

Chapter: 6: Your Inner Voice Helps You Self-Regulate

Imagine this: You're standing at the edge of a cliff, looking down at the turbulent waves crashing against the rocks below. Your heart races, your palms get sweaty, and an overwhelming sense of anxiety washes over you. But what if I told you that there's a simple technique, grounded in psychological research, that can help you find calm amidst the chaos?

In a groundbreaking study titled "Self-Talk as a Regulatory Mechanism: How You Do It Matters," conducted by Kross et al. in 2014, researchers delved into the fascinating realm of self-talk and its impact on our emotions and behaviors, particularly in the face of social stress. They discovered that the way we address ourselves internally during introspection can make all the difference in how we navigate distressing situations.

The Power of Mental Distance

When you find yourself dealing with anxiety or distressing situations, mentally step back and view the situation as if you were an external observer. Think of it as a mental zoom-out button. This technique, known as self-distancing, involves shifting from first-person pronouns ("I" or "me") to non-first-person pronouns ("you," "he," "she," or even your own name). By doing so, you create psychological distance, allowing you to approach the situation with a more objective and detached perspective.

So, instead of saying, "I'm having a panic attack. I'm going to faint here on this cliff edge, and everyone is going to see," you say, "You've got this, Emily. You're experiencing some panic right now, but you're safe. You're not going to faint."

You can probably tell the difference, right? The first feels so much more personal, threatening, and non-negotiable.

The second makes the situation seem much more manageable somehow.

Imagine you're preparing to give a presentation at work. The mere thought of it makes your heart race and your mind run through worst-case scenarios. Instead of getting trapped in the whirlwind of your own emotions, step back and address yourself as if you were coaching someone else: "All right, [Your Name], you've got this. Remember to take deep breaths, speak clearly, and engage the audience. You've done your research, and you're well-prepared."

By employing this technique, you're giving yourself the space to see the situation from a different angle. It's like watching a movie of your life rather than being lost in the script. This newfound perspective can diminish the intensity of your emotional response, helping you think more clearly and act with greater composure. Essentially, you've created "psychological distance." You're no longer fused with scary and overwhelming thoughts—you're standing at some distance away from them, and that makes them easier to handle.

Remember, anxiety narrows your focus so that when you're so immersed in your own thoughts and feelings, you lose perspective. Self-distancing is your antidote to this tunnel vision. It empowers you to regain control over your thoughts and emotions, making you more resilient in the face of anxiety-provoking moments.

Becoming Your Own Coach

When you're faced with challenges or striving toward your goals, embrace the role of a supportive coach within your own mind. Just as a coach provides guidance, motivation, and constructive feedback to help an athlete excel, you can guide yourself through life's hurdles with the same positivity and wisdom.

Imagine you're embarking on a journey to improve your public speaking skills. Instead of letting self-doubt and negative thoughts dictate your narrative, step into the coach's shoes: "All right, Nick, today's your chance to practice and grow. Remember, every great speaker started somewhere. Focus on your strengths, maintain eye contact, and let your passion shine through. And hey, even if you stumble a bit, it's all part of the learning process. You're making progress, and I'm here to support you every step of the way."

This shift in self-talk isn't about sugarcoating challenges or ignoring areas for improvement. It's about fostering a kind, motivating, and empowering relationship with yourself, just as a coach does with their team. When you adopt this approach, you're not just offering yourself empty words of encouragement; you're establishing a growth-oriented mindset that fuels your journey forward.

Rather than succumbing to the spiraling thoughts of "I can't do this" or "I'm not good enough," redirect your inner dialogue. Allow it to support you, guide you, and encourage you.

"All right, the first thing is just to break the task down."

"Stay focused—you know how to do this."

"Breathe."

"You've beaten obstacles before, and you can beat this one, too."

"Keep your head up and square your shoulders."

"You're doing great. Keep going!"

By speaking to yourself as a coach, you're creating a nurturing and empowering mental environment. Just as a coach celebrates successes and guides through setbacks, you're fostering resilience, self-belief, and a more present mindset. In a world often filled with noise and self-doubt, let your internal coach be the steady, motivating force that propels you forward with confidence and clarity.

Chapter 7: Feeling Depressed? Be Kind

"Healing through Helping: An Experimental Investigation of Kindness, Social Activities, and Reappraisal as Well-Being Interventions," a collaborative effort by David R. Cregg and Jennifer S. Cheavens, is more than just a study—it's a compass pointing us toward a mental landscape that's less stormy and more serene, a terrain where the power of kindness and the act of helping others reign supreme.

While it may seem counterintuitive to some, helping others may turn out to be the most reliable way of helping ourselves. It could be that the corollary is also true: Relentless self-focus is the fast-track way to unhappiness.

Acts of Kindness as Cognitive Control

By shifting your attention toward helping others, you may experience improvements in your own mental well-being. It sounds nice, but why should this be the case?

We've already seen that engaging actively with the present brings us out of our minds and out of endless impotent rumination. Engaging in acts of kindness, however, can also serve as a form of cognitive control, allowing you to redirect your thoughts and emotions in a positive and constructive manner. It can be difficult to stay grounded and pragmatic when caught up in our own neuroses—but it's easier to see the way forward when it comes to other people. Kindness, then, is *simple*.

Consider the story of Emily, who, amidst her own struggles with anxiety, started writing letters of encouragement to hospital patients. As she penned heartfelt words to uplift others, she found herself less entangled in her own anxious thoughts. Simply, all that anxious mental energy was put to some real use in the world. It was channeled and directed. Emily not only felt less alone, but she was distracting herself from useless ruminations, finding a purpose, and increasing her self-efficacy.

So, the next time you find yourself mired in negativity, extend a helping hand—it might just be the lifeline you need. You may find even more paradoxical benefit in giving to others what you most feel you lack. If you're lonely, volunteer to help with isolated older folks trapped indoors. If you're feeling unloved, work at the orphanage. If you're feeling directionless in life, offer to coach wayward teens at a summer camp. You get the idea.

Consider the butterfly effect of kindness. When Daniel, a teacher dealing with chronic anxiety, decided to start a small scholarship fund for his students, he couldn't have foreseen the ripple of positivity it would create. Not only did he provide opportunities for his students, but he also experienced a remarkable shift in his own well-being. The act of contributing to others' futures acted as a magnetic force, pulling his attention away from anxious thoughts and directing it toward a brighter, altruistic focus.

Remember, acts of kindness need not be grand gestures to yield transformative effects. You don't have to do something flashy or work with a major organization in an impoverished country. Just look around your world and see who is struggling.

Struggling with depression, Jane decided to challenge herself: She would express gratitude to a different person every day. Whether it was a heartfelt note or a simple text, Jane's commitment to spreading positivity not only uplifted others but rewired her own thought patterns. She was suddenly aware of just how blessed she was and how many kind, well-meaning people surrounded her. As she shifted her attention toward brightening others' days, her own days began to shine a little brighter as well.

Finding Purpose and Fulfillment through Helping Others

Anxious minds can be like labyrinths. You don't want to turn continually inward and get further trapped in the maze. Instead, allow kindness to help you turn outward into the world and into connections with others—who, it won't be a big surprise, struggle just the same as you do.

Helping others can give you a sense of purpose, meaning, fulfillment, and satisfaction that can lower your stress. One afternoon of meaningfully connecting with other human beings can be more powerful than six months spent in therapy, churning endlessly over the same old stories of trauma and victimization.

Meet Sam, a father striving to balance the demands of his job and family life. Feeling like a hamster on a wheel, he found solace in mentoring a group of teenagers in his community. As he shared his experiences and insights, he discovered many things:

- That he knew a lot more than he thought he did—in fact, he possessed loads of wisdom and experience that others needed and wanted.
- That he felt an enormous sense of satisfaction by contributing to the growth and development of young people.
- That, to put it bluntly, his life was challenging but it could have been a lot worse! Grumbling about his family took on a fresh perspective when he worked closely with kids who never knew what it was to have a family and never had the privileges he did.

- That just as these kids struggled but would work things out, he, too, would have difficulty with his life stage, but he'd learn and grow, too.
- That at the end of the day, the value of life was not in the next paycheck, but in being a person of virtue, in connecting with others, and in being a force of good in the world. This gave Sam more resilience and determination than he believed possible.

The act of helping them navigate life's challenges provided a perspective that shifted his own worries into the background. This narrative echoes the study's conclusion—when you're engaged in assisting others, you're simultaneously anchoring yourself in the present and gaining a renewed sense of purpose.

Think about the last time you performed an act of kindness, whether it was a small gesture like holding the door for someone, or a more substantial effort like volunteering at a local shelter. Remember the warmth that spread within you, the feeling of contributing to someone's happiness. You immediately felt like you wanted to do more, right? This sense of fulfillment is like a balm for your mind, a countermeasure to the turmoil of overthinking and anxiety. It's a reminder that there's more to life than the worries that often consume us.

Chapter 8: The Good News in Bad News

In a world where we're bombarded with negative news headlines and distressing information at every turn, it's easy to feel overwhelmed and anxious. However, recent research conducted by Tel Aviv University's School of Psychological Sciences sheds light on an intriguing phenomenon that can help us navigate the turbulent seas of negativity and regain control of our emotions and cognitive abilities. The study suggests that repeated exposure to negative events can have a surprising impact on our mood and cognitive functions.

Building Resilience through Negative Visualization

Imagine this scenario: You wake up one morning to a barrage of unsettling news headlines, and your mood takes a nosedive. Your mind races with worst-case scenarios, envisioning a bleak future filled with challenges, losses, and setbacks. Sound familiar? This is where the first tip comes into play: negative visualization. Instead of shying away from these distressing thoughts, embrace them. Picture those potential challenges vividly, as if they were unfolding before your eyes.

By repeatedly imagining these realistic negative scenarios, you're doing more than just acknowledging their existence—you're taking control of your emotional response. The Tel Aviv University study reveals that initially, exposure to negative information can indeed put you in a bad mood and impair your cognitive abilities. Through repetition, however, something remarkable happens. These negative scenarios begin to lose their emotional grip on you, resulting in an improved mood and enhanced cognitive performance. In other words, you are becoming desensitized to them.

Naturally, this study isn't permission to consume hours of mood-damaging online content—most of which is not necessary or beneficial. Rather, it's pointing to the fact that sometimes, our anxiety makes us mentally pull back from certain situations we've convinced ourselves are unbearable. But by strenuously avoiding and fearing this fear, we only give it more power.

Imagine you are eaten up with worry over your marriage. Things aren't great, and you are unable to sleep at night stewing over the thought that your spouse is going to file for divorce, leaving you sad, alone, and a little poorer to boot. This thought is so unbearable that the more you stress about it, the more it seems to hurt—and the more you stress about it.

Unfortunately, just lying in bed, ruminating on "What if I get divorced?" over and over is not likely to have therapeutic effects. Rather, face the fear head on. Typically, you'll notice that your mind stops at a certain point—but push it onward and follow it through. This will help you engage with and eventually counteract "catastrophizing."

"What if I get divorced?"

"Well, so what if you do?"

"I'll be sad and all alone, and it'll leave me destitute, too."

"Okay . . . and *then what*?"

Notice that this pushes you past your point of catastrophe—the point at which your mind can't even bear to go further.

"Well . . . then I suppose I'll be all alone. I'll have to go live in some crummy apartment for a while and lick my wounds."

"You'll be sad for a while. How long?"

"I don't know. A year? Two?"

"And what happens after two years?"

"Well, I guess I'll start moving on eventually . . . but I'll still be sad."

"Of course you will be. But will it be the end of the world?"

"No, it won't be the end of the world . . . It'll just be really difficult."

"But you would survive it. You'd move on, and in a few years, you'd be doing something else."

"I guess so."

As you can see, the authors of the study are not suggesting that you do more endless catastrophizing. Instead, they're pointing to the act of de-catastrophizing and taking some of the power out of your "worst-case scenarios."

Every day, set aside a few minutes to visualize the worst-case scenarios you're worried about. Picture missing a crucial deadline, making a significant mistake, or being rejected or humiliated. Don't pull any punches.

At first, it will feel uncomfortable. But as you persist, notice how this discomfort is really not the end of the world. Notice how, as you get familiar with a scenario, it loses some of its emotional power. Notice that you can survive it, even if it is unpleasant. Notice that life can and will go on, even if the most unthinkable thing comes to pass. This is what makes you more resilient.

Embracing Voluntary Hardships

Cold showers, insanely early mornings, fasting, deliberately delayed gratification . . . some people use these things to increase their happiness.

This might sound counterintuitive—why would you willingly add discomfort to your life? However, the goal is not masochism but to build resilience, become more present, and reduce anxiety and overthinking.

Begin with simple challenges, such as taking cold showers or practicing intermittent fasting. These might seem like minor inconveniences, but they can have a profound impact on your mental fortitude. Cold showers, for instance, force you to confront discomfort and focus your mind on the present moment. Likewise, intermittent fasting challenges your impulse control and helps you develop a deeper connection with your body's signals.

As you become more comfortable with these manageable hardships, gradually increase the difficulty. Perhaps you can take on more extended fasts or expose yourself to even colder temperatures. By willingly subjecting yourself to these challenges, you're training your mind to adapt and stay present in the face of adversity. Even more importantly, you're teaching yourself that *adversity is temporary*, and that you can survive it—in fact, it can make you stronger, more grateful, more focused.

Let me tell a story about my cousin Mike. He's a software engineer plagued by constant overthinking and anxiety, and he decided to implement the concept of manageable voluntary hardships in his life. He started with something as simple as a daily cold shower. The first few days were excruciating—the shock of cold water on his skin sent shivers down his spine. But he persisted. With each cold shower, he focused on his breath, learning to embrace discomfort instead of resisting it.

As weeks turned into months, Mike's capacity to handle discomfort grew. He no longer dreaded the cold shower; instead, it became a meditative practice that allowed him to stay grounded and present. Encouraged by his progress, he decided to tackle intermittent fasting. Skipping breakfast and extending his fasting window challenged his cravings and taught him to listen to his body's hunger cues.

Mike's journey wasn't about seeking unnecessary suffering; it was about deliberately introducing challenges to build mental resilience. Over time, he found himself less anxious, his overthinking had diminished, and he was better equipped to handle life's uncertainties. As a nice side effect, he noticed he was able to quit smoking—because he had trained himself to ride out discomfort and craving and come out the other end unbothered. What could you use that skill for in your own life?

Chapter 9: Mindful Movement Lowers Stress

Cultivating Mental Clarity

While on a tranquil walk through the woods, you're surrounded by lush greenery, the gentle rustling of leaves, and the joyful chirping of birds. Instead of your mind being consumed by your never-ending to-do list or the stress of upcoming deadlines, you consciously choose to focus on the present moment. Your senses awaken as you feel the cool breeze on your skin, hear the rhythmic sound of your footsteps, and catch the subtle scent of nature in the air. This is what we mean when we talk about mindfulness in action.

A recent study found that individuals, especially college students, experienced reduced stress and negative emotions when they practiced mindfulness while moving, such as walking. By immersing themselves in the present, they were able to get out of their heads and into their bodies.

The next time you're walking to a meeting or even just from your car to your workplace, try this: Focus on your breath and the sensation of each step. Notice the sights and sounds around you. Feel the ground beneath your feet. This intentional act of presence can help clear your mind and provide a respite from the mental chatter.

If (or shall we say, when) your mental chatter erupts again, that's no problem—just notice it, take a breath, and bring your attention back to what's going on in this very moment, right now. Tell yourself that whatever it is, it can wait. All those worries and thoughts will still be there when you return from your walk, if you still want to chew over them! Use your five senses to help anchor and ground you. When you catch your mind going off the rails, go back to your senses:

- What can you smell? The clean, sweetish scent of autumn leaves on cold ground? Rain coming?
- Look around you—notice the subtle shades of different colors all on the same leaf, or the way the light is dappled at the foot of a tree.
- What sounds can you hear? Listen even more closely—what can you hear when you *really* listen?
  What does it actually feel like to walk, to stand upright, to have the solidity of the ground underneath your feet? Pluck a stem of grass—how does its stalk feel against your fingertips?
- Yes, you can even enlist taste on your walk—have you ever chewed on the end of a piece of sweet grass? What if you brought a little snack with you and savored it, one bite at a time?
- The senses go beyond just five, though. Try to feel the quality of the air and light around you. Get a sense of being inside a landscape, become aware of how the elements are interacting with one another, and how you yourself are one of those elements, moving with the flow.

Slow and Intentional Movement Magic

There is power in embracing deliberate, unhurried movements while staying tuned in to your breath. This dynamic duo sends a clear signal to your nervous system, activating the parasympathetic response, aka the "rest and digest" mode. In our turbocharged lives, it's easy to get caught up in the sympathetic "fight-or-flight" mode, and that can pave the way for chronic stress and anxiety.

Try to think about yourself on a bad day. Maybe you're seated at your desk, shoulders hunched, and your mind is a whirlwind of worries. Now, instead of staying in that anxious state, what if you took a moment to sit up straight, close your eyes, and take a deep, calming breath? As you breathe in and out, feel the tension slowly releasing. And as you go about your next movement, whether it's a stretch, a yoga pose, or simply reaching for a glass of water, what if you did it deliberately, fully attuned to the rhythm of your body and your breath?

In the study, the participants who combined mindfulness with physical activity reported a remarkable boost in their well-being. This intentional blend of movement and breath not only helps you connect with your body but also soothes the anxious mind. It's a simple yet effective way to shift from a state of constant worry to one of calm and presence.

Formal sitting meditation is not necessary. Simply add little "windows" of mindfulness all throughout the day. A stretch here, a breath there. A walk, a smile, a moment of restful contemplation. Infusing mindfulness into your everyday routines can truly revolutionize your life. You'll find your mind clearing, anxiety taking a back seat, and a sense of well-being settling in. And all you need to get started is here already: your breath, your body, and the ever-unfolding present moment.

Chapter 10: Bothered by Negative, Unwanted Thoughts? Just Throw Them Away

Recent research conducted at Ohio State University delves into the captivating realm of thought management, yielding enlightening insights. The truth is, not all thoughts are created equal. Some are useful, some are partially useful . . . and some are just plain old garbage. If you have a garbage thought that you can't seem to get rid of, this chapter has some tips for detaching and getting on with your life.

Transforming Thoughts into Tangible Entities

The first tip, which revolves around the practice of writing down negative thoughts, is a simple yet profoundly effective strategy for managing our mental landscape. This technique involves externalizing those troublesome thoughts by transferring them from the swirling depths of our mind onto a tangible medium, such as a piece of paper or a digital note. Again, we see the power of creating psychological distance and detaching ourselves from harmful thoughts. By physically manifesting these thoughts, we create perspective and objectivity.

During my teenage years, I embarked on a creative journey by writing a manuscript that I hoped would someday become a published novel. As is often the case with creative endeavors, however, I frequently found myself grappling with intense self-doubt. It was during these moments that I felt my manuscript would never be good enough, and this persistent negativity threatened to undermine my passion for writing.

Then, I discovered the power of externalization through writing. One day, as I sat in my dimly lit room, doubting the worth of my manuscript, I decided to put pen to paper. I started jotting down every self-critical thought that plagued me. It was as if I was transferring the weight of my doubts from my mind onto the page before me. As I saw my negative thoughts in black and white, something transformative happened. I saw the thoughts, now outside of myself. They were pretty rotten. Had I really been carrying all *that* around my whole life?

Once the thoughts were out there, it seemed so much easier to engage with them. After all, they were just words, whereas in my head, they had felt like absolute objective reality. I took my pen to the words themselves and realized I could "edit" them in exactly the same way as I had edited my own manuscript. I took a red pen and went to work correcting them. Actually, after a few minutes I had a breakthrough—*nothing* that I had written on the paper had any value. There was nothing to edit—it was all garbage. I crumbled up the piece of paper and threw it away.

I began to view my manuscript more objectively. I realized that the harsh critiques I'd been subjecting myself to were just that—self-imposed and unnecessarily harsh. By externalizing these thoughts, I could scrutinize them from a distance. I noticed patterns in my thinking, like my tendency to magnify flaws and underestimate the strengths of my work. Those thoughts popped back up, but I no longer took them as seriously. "What are you doing here? Aren't you supposed to be in the bin?"

Promoting Cognitive Flexibility

This practice disrupts the repetitive and rigid thought patterns that often plague our minds, creating room for alternative perspectives and healthier cognitive processing.

Imagine a scenario where you find yourself trapped in a cycle of overthinking and anxiety, constantly worrying about an upcoming presentation at work or a challenging exam. These thoughts consume your mental energy, leaving you feeling overwhelmed and stressed. You begin by writing down these thoughts as they arise, acknowledging them without judgment.

Next comes the transformative step: discarding these written thoughts. It's akin to symbolically letting go of the worries that have been weighing you down. You might tear up the paper, crumple it into a ball, or simply throw it away (maybe if you're feeling dramatic, you burn it).

The power of this technique lies in its ability to interrupt the repetitive and unproductive thought patterns that contribute to anxiety and overthinking. You disrupt the old loops that keep anxiety cycling in your mind. This provides a mental pause, creating an opportunity to consider alternative perspectives or simply allow your mind to rest.

Chapter 11: Take that Leap—Do Something!

"Nothing diminishes anxiety faster than action." — Walter Anderson

Now, let's turn our attention to the profound wisdom of Walter Anderson as our guiding star. His insights illuminate a simple truth: As we take tangible steps toward our dreams, not only do we evade the pitfalls of procrastination, but we also release the tight grip of anxiety that's been holding us hostage.

Think of it this way: Thought and action are two mutually exclusive modes and cannot occupy one entity at the same time. If you're acting, you're not thinking. If you're thinking, you're not acting. This is why people say things like, "I was terrified at first, but once we got started, it was all okay and I even started to enjoy it after a while."

Creating a Positive Feedback Loop

Imagine, for a moment, the classic quest for better health. When you commit to regular exercise and healthy eating, you embark on a transformational journey. Your body begins to change, and you start to feel good. Each workout or nutritious meal becomes proof that you are in charge of your health, and that you can take control and do better, one choice at a time, one day at a time.

Alex dreamed of becoming a writer, but she was initially plagued by self-doubt. She questioned whether becoming a published author was merely a distant fantasy. She questioned a lot actually: whether she had any real talent, whether print media was dead, whether people would make fun of her, whether to write YA fiction or work on her first love—poetry. But Alex was able to see that after all this worry, one thing was not getting done: writing. She decided that all she would focus on was writing. That was all. She committed to writing at least three hundred words a day, rain or shine. She ignored all the other head noise.

As time unfolded, those words blossomed into articles and essays, much like a garden flourishing under the gentle sunlight. And then, the moment of truth arrived when Alex's work got published and accolades poured in. Did she immediately win a Nobel Prize and become a millionaire? No, of course not. But she kept on taking action day after day, and her writing career developed. One thing is for sure—even if she only made modest advances, she still went infinitely further than she would have by just sitting at home, paralyzed, unable to do more than worry.

Remember, if you want to be the hero of your story, then action has to be your superpower!

Diminishing Your Anxiety's Power through Action

Imagine telling anxiety, "Not today, my friend!"

Let me share a personal story with you. Back in the day, I harbored a fear of starting my own business. It felt like tiptoeing through a field of uncertainty. But I made a conscious choice to confront this fear head-on. It wasn't all smooth sailing, but every successful business move felt like a small victory chipping away at my anxiety. As I witnessed my business thrive and my confidence soar, I not only conquered my fear but also reveled in the exhilaration of entrepreneurship.

One way to start doing this for yourself is to convert worries directly into either actions or questions. For example:

"I'm worried that I'll run out of savings before I start turning a profit."

We can turn this into a question to start with:

"Will I run out of savings before I start turning a profit?"

The only real answer to this is "I don't know." Immediately we get some psychological distance and challenge our all-or-nothing thinking. Let's go further and use this question to help us generate real actions we can take in our world today:

"How much savings do I actually have?"
"How long will that last me?"
"How can I make it last longer?"
"What can I do to start turning a profit sooner?"

Already, our fear has been transformed into something far more useful. After thinking (not worrying) about these questions for a while, you decide to take some concrete steps:

1. Consolidate all your available savings so you know what you're working with
2. Calculate a bare-minimum budget
3. See how long your savings will last you, given this budget
4. Start to investigate ways to launch your business sooner, and start getting some income

Now, you don't have to worry. You just have to act. If you sit with a worry and find you can't mine it for any value as an action, then you know what to do: Get rid of it!

The next time you face a fear that's been holding you back, remember this: Action is a weapon against anxiety. Conquer any fear lurking in the shadows of your heart with unwavering determination. You are the author of your story, and every action you take is a brushstroke on the canvas of your extraordinary life.

Chapter 12: The Wisdom of "So What?"

"I just give myself permission to suck... I find this hugely liberating." —John Green

So, let me be your guide to the enigmatic world of John Green, the illustrious author of *The Fault in Our Stars*. His words aren't mere pearls of wisdom; they're like the playful nudges of a mischievous mentor, inviting us to embark on a journey less ordinary—a journey paved with the beautiful imperfections of life.

Embracing Intentional Failure

Imagine this: A budding artist stands before a blank canvas. Instead of trembling at the thought of every brushstroke, they wield their brushes with an air of audacity. They're like a magician conjuring colors onto the canvas. They know deep down that not every stroke will be a masterpiece. Some might even resemble a surrealist's interpretation of spaghetti. But here's what matters—they're painting. They're doing it. They're not letting fear shape their lives.

Let me introduce you to John. He's painfully shy and believes at a core level that rejection just might kill him. John wants more than anything to meet a nice girl and have a relationship, but he's petrified that women will reject him. He's taken all the advice dished out by dating coaches, but it only seems to make things worse. That's because, underneath it all, their underlying message is just more of the same: be confident, be slick, be cool.

John discovers that the opposite is actually true. One day his friend asks him, "What are you even afraid of? So a woman turns you down, big deal. The worst that can happen is that some girl out there thinks you're terrible.

Who cares?" It's a lightbulb moment for John. His trouble, he sees, is not that he's unable to be confident. It's that he's *unable to be a failure.*

So he sets himself a task. He goes out one morning with one agenda: chat with at least fifty girls and deliberately get rejected by each of them. You'll recognize elements of desensitization in this plan to deliberately fail, but there's more. John goes out, chats with a few girls, and they all politely turn him down. Much to his surprise, it's nowhere near as awful as he always thought it would be. In fact, getting rejected quickly feels . . . kind of boring and ordinary.

Now, I'm not going to say that the fiftieth girl was so charmed she immediately fell in love with him (this isn't a rom com!), but I will say that in the weeks following this experiment, something changed in John. He had given himself permission to be imperfect. Permission to not have everyone like him. Permission to be a flawed human being with fears and weaknesses. Permission to go out into the world and engage with it, even if it got a little scary at times.

With this new mindset, he finds that he's more confident, more relaxed, and less fearful. And—you guessed it—it's this attitude that starts to make him more attractive to others, and a girlfriend isn't far behind. Women end up drawn to John *not* because he's cool and confident—but because he's human, he's real, and he's unafraid to be vulnerable. Plus, he's a lot of fun!

John Green's wisdom serves as a reminder that life is an exquisite canvas, and the pursuit of personal excellence becomes an art form when we liberate ourselves from the chains of perfectionism. By embracing intentional failure, we don't just paint a picture; we create a masterpiece of resilience and growth, all while savoring the quirky, unexpected beauty of our imperfections.

Process > Outcome

When's the last time you found yourself at the theater, bubbling with anticipation for the latest blockbuster? You've got your popcorn and a soda the size of a small car, and your heart is practically tap dancing with excitement. But here's the million-dollar question: Do you slyly slip in just as the closing credits are about to roll, all to claim you were there at the finish line? Or are you the type who relishes every frame, from the opening scene to the grand finale, like a movie maestro soaking in the nuances of a cinematic masterpiece?

Life is just like savoring a cinematic adventure. Think of yourself as the director of your own epic blockbuster, with each day being a new scene in the script of your life. Instead of fixating solely on how the story concludes, why not relish the exhilarating process of crafting every scene? It's about embracing the plot twists, the character development, and the unexpected adventures that come your way.

Allow me to introduce you to Mike, my high-achieving colleague, who was once the embodiment of perfectionism. He'd agonize over the smallest details, like ensuring his collection of rare antique rubber ducks stood in perfect formation. Yes, rubber ducks, you read that correctly!

Now, Mike decided it was time to flip the script on his own life's movie. He shifted his focus from anxiously awaiting the grand finale to appreciating the marvelous journey. No longer did he fixate on reaching the end credits with everything perfectly in place. Instead, he cherished the process—the plot twists, the character growth (including, you guessed it, his rubber ducks), and the invaluable life lessons he encountered along the way.

By adopting this process-oriented mindset, Mike didn't just dial down his anxiety; he discovered that the thrill of the journey was far more exhilarating than the elusive mirage of a perfect ending.

Chapter 13: The Past Is Gone

"What is the point of dragging up sufferings that are over, of being miserable now, because you were miserable then?" —Seneca

Have you ever felt stuck in a cycle of revisiting old wounds and past mistakes? We've all been there, but here's a question to ponder: What's the point?

Seneca reminds us that there's little benefit in dwelling on past pain to the point where it affects our current happiness. Instead, Seneca encourages us to shift our focus to the present moment and the actions we can take now to improve our current circumstances.

There is a funny saying that goes, "I can't be happy until my parents treated me better as a child." It's a nonsense statement that highlights the futility of stewing over what literally cannot be changed. The Stoics were famous for their clear-headed understanding of the difference between what can be changed and what cannot. Any dwelling on what cannot be changed is just recreational misery—and it takes away energy that could be more fruitfully directed at something you *could* change.

In practical terms, it means acknowledging our past experiences without letting them define or dictate our present emotions and choices. It's a call to release the weight of yesterday's burdens and embrace the potential and opportunities of today. By doing so, we can cultivate a more mindful, purposeful, and contented existence.

Releasing the Past

Have you ever found yourself lost in the maze of past regrets and mishaps, replaying them like a broken record?

Trust me, I've been down that rabbit hole too, and it's a bit like trying to catch smoke with a butterfly net. I began asking questions that are literally unanswerable:

"Why me?"
"Why is life so unfair?"
"Why did I do X when I could have done Y?"
"Why can't this be easier?"

I heard someone once say that *why* should be an acronym for Won't Help You. Take a look:

"I was bullied relentlessly in high school. Why do people like that always get away with it?"

What is an appropriate response to the above? There is no real answer because this is not a real question—it's just an invitation to ruminate and go down a negative rabbit hole:

"They get away with it because the teachers don't care, that's why. Let's be realistic—they're not getting paid enough to care, so they turn a blind eye. And parents don't want to rock the boat. So the whole thing's set up against the kid being bullied. I suppose it's a good lesson in a way, because when you grow up, the adult world is just as full of bullies, and there's just one long line of bullies after the first one, each of them doing whatever they want with impunity..."

So, we started with a single incident of bulling in the past (which is, let's remember, *over*) and extended that bad feeling to include all teachers everywhere at all times, all adults, the entire workplace, and basically one hundred percent of humanity with everything in it—past, future, and for all time. Not to mention that with this mental filter on, you swiftly ignore the many great people you currently work with, the teachers who were kind to you at school, your many achievements, your caring parents, even the many times that *you* were the one doing the bullying . . .

All this line of thinking has achieved is to cement in your mind your role as an eternal victim. Not very empowering, is it?

A profound shift in perspective is needed—an acknowledgment that past experiences, no matter how cringe-worthy or unfair or horrible, have contributed to shaping your life today. And what's more, you are always at liberty to be different, feel different, and choose different, right here and right now.

Once I learned to keep the past in the past, it was like a lightbulb had gone off. Regret, my constant companion, began to fade into the background. Self-pity started to lose its grip.
With each passing day, I nurtured a positive mindset rooted in the lessons I had gleaned from my past blunders. And for those experiences that were not my fault, I did my best to let go.

Mindful Awareness and Present Peace

Next, let's talk about the power of mindfulness in breaking free from the ceaseless cycle of rumination.

I distinctly remember a phase in my life when I was in the grip of overthinking about a past failure. I had been given a chance, and I blew it—can you relate? No matter how bad and embarrassed I felt, the deed was done and the consequences unfolded. I was wracked with guilt and remorse, and beat myself up for what I'd done. We've all been there, unfortunately.

It was like being caught in quicksand, each anxious thought dragging me deeper into the muck, stealing away precious moments in the present. Seneca's question came to me:

"What is the point of dragging up sufferings that are over?"

In the moment it seemed cruel and irrelevant. My mind retorted with a thousand reasons why I needed to keep thinking about this disaster over and over again. But at the end was always the same question. "Does all this thinking help? Has all that worrying done a single thing to undo what has already been done?"

The answer, of course, was no. And then from that it was clear: I was making myself unhappy, *and for no good reason*. So, if the past was always going to be the past whether I worried about it or not, I might as well choose not, right?

Gradually, I was forced to learn to observe my thoughts and emotions without judgment. When the specters of past hardships loomed, I became adept at recognizing them for what they were: no longer angry and vengeful ghosts from the past, but tired old reruns from a show I'd seen so many times I was getting bored of it!

Mindfulness was my sturdy anchor to the present. I engaged in practices such as meditation and deep breathing to tether myself to the here and now. Gradually, serenity, a precious rarity, became a cherished companion. By staying attuned to my thoughts and gently steering them away from the turbulent waters of the past, I not only regained mastery over my mind but also over my life.

Chapter 14: Drop the Blame

"When we feel bad, we often automatically decide that either we are bad or another person is bad. Both of these moves cause damage and distort the truth, which is that we are all navigating difficult conditions the best we can, and we all have a lot to learn and unlearn." —Dean Spade

Compare the following:

1. "I feel hurt."
2. "You hurt me."

Take a moment to think about the differences between the two sentiments above.

We often find ourselves caught in the blame game. Something is wrong, so we look for the person who did it, acting like detectives eagerly assigning fault to the nearest suspect—be it ourselves or an unwitting bystander.

When the going gets tough, we tend to slap labels on ourselves or others in a bid to make sense of our own experiences. If there's a victim, there's got to be a villain, right?

If you're caught in anxious rumination, try to let go of the need to find someone who is responsible. Remind yourself that even if you do, blaming them—or even punishing them—brings you closer to what you really desire. Instead, focus on the present, focus on solutions, and focus on what you can do here and now to make things better. That means resisting the urge to wallow in self-recrimination, but also the urge to get trapped complaining about others as getting a little too much enjoyment out of being the victim.

Your Unrealistic Expectations

First, let's hit the brakes before we impulsively leap to conclusions about our inherent virtue or vice. Life is often way, way more complicated than that.

Let me share a personal story. I once found myself ensnared in the intricate web of self-doubt and blame after a project at work took an unexpected nosedive. I was poised to cast myself as the "villain" in this unfolding drama. It took a lot of introspection to finally gain some clarity.

I took a deliberate breath and reached for my journal. I meticulously began documenting the details of the situation that had left me feeling so confused and upset. I listed the steps I had taken along the winding path that had led to this challenging crossroads.

This practice enabled me to objectively assess the nature of my actions, discerning whether they had truly fallen within the sphere of my influence. Upon careful reflection, I recognized that my choices had indeed played a role, but not *all* of them were bad. Gradually I turned black-and-white thinking into shades of gray.

I asked myself some key questions:

What was under my control in the past?
What is under my control right now?
What can I no longer do anything to change?
What can I do right now to improve the situation?
What do I need to forgive, in myself and others?
What lesson can I learn from all this?
What do I need to DO now to move on?

In other words, instead of *fault*, think in terms of control. What is in your control and what isn't? What can be changed and what can't? That's a good place to start.

I realized that although I was somewhat to blame, there was no point dwelling on myself as a villain. Rather, I needed to redeem the situation by making pragmatic changes and learning the lessons I could. I made a swift apology and immediately got to work making sure the same misunderstandings wouldn't happen again.

None of this could have been achieved if I had stayed fixated on identifying the good guys and bad guys in the story. Spoiler alert: we are all, to some degree, good guys *and* bad guys.

The quote serves as a poignant reminder that kindness toward oneself and the acknowledgment of our limitations are the foundational steppingstones to personal growth and emotional well-being. As we continue our intricate dance through life's twists and turns, may we find solace in the profound wisdom of introspection and the graceful embrace of self-compassion.

The Power of Empathy

As Spade's quote brilliantly reminds us, beneath our everyday actions and reactions lies a shared human struggle. Blaming and black-and-white thinking feels like an easy way to make sense of messy situations, but it's just not a reliable way to navigate life. The reality is, we're all navigating a maze of intricate circumstances, each with our own unique set of challenges.

Jeffrey once found himself caught in a web of workplace drama. Frustration and resentment threatened to consume him, leading to a potential judgmental verdict on a colleague. However, Jeffrey decided to resist the urge to villainize the other person. Instead of leaping to conclusions, he made a conscious effort to step into his colleague's shoes, imagining the pressures, demands, and intricacies of his life. Suddenly, instead of judgment, he felt himself approaching the situation with curiosity—which is the very first step of compassion and empathy.

As Jeffrey engaged in a role-reversal thought experiment, the landscape began to shift. He discovered that his colleague was actually dealing with his mother's death. This newfound understanding paved the way for a more compassionate approach, ultimately fostering a significant improvement in the working relationship.

Now, this didn't magically make the conflict disappear, but what it did do is open up an opportunity to start really engaging with the problem. Jeffrey and his colleague could sit down together and start a conversation, putting concrete steps into action instead of quietly fuming at one another. Jeffrey not only transformed their workplace interactions but also underwent a profound shift in his own mindset, discovering that he felt much less inclined to be critical of his own mistakes.

Chapter 15: Needs Versus Wants

"Distinguish between real needs and artificial wants and control the latter." —Mahatma Gandhi

We reside in a world where we're bombarded daily with messages clamoring for "more, more, more," and it's all too easy to get swept away. By embracing Gandhi's wisdom, you can master the art of distinguishing between your genuine needs and the glittering nonsense that disguises itself as need. By developing a mature discernment about what is and isn't necessary, you can also teach yourself to surf through waves of your cravings.

Artificial Wants Versus Real Needs

Think of your life as a ship embarking on the boundless expanse of existence. The sustenance of your well-being, akin to the cargo aboard this vessel, hinges upon a precarious equilibrium. Within this cargo, you'll find your authentic needs: sustenance, shelter, water, and human connections. These are the fundamental provisions that not only sustain your journey but ensure its smooth sailing.

In contrast, there exists another facet of this cargo—the artificial desires. This is the excess baggage heaped upon your vessel by society, relentless advertising, and the pressures of peers. These desires can manifest as material possessions, symbols of status, or the relentless pursuit of external validation. These superfluous desires, however enticing, can encumber your voyage, rendering your ship sluggish and susceptible to turbulence—or sinking.

Consider a luxury car. It's expensive, it's sexy, it's glossy and high-end. But how much of that glamor genuinely serves a purpose? Will it truly elevate your well-being, or is it merely an artificial craving fanned by societal expectations?

Now imagine all the worry and anxiety that comes with having that car. It needs constant maintenance (if it breaks down, they have to order special replacement parts from Germany that cost the same as a small secondhand car) and a place to park it so it's safe, and you're constantly stressed that the car wash is going to damage the special paint finish. This is not to mention the cost of buying or renting it.

"But what am I supposed to do? I need a car, right?"

That may be true, but do you need *that* car?

Here's a simpler explanation for when *need* tips over into *want*. Let's say you have a glass on a table, and you're thirsty. Someone pours you a drink of water. A half glass is great and definitely welcome. Still, it would be nice to have a full glass so your thirst is completely quenched. So you ask the person to pour some more. They pour a full glass—that's great!—but they continue pouring. The water reaches the top rim and then overflows. They keep pouring. Pretty soon you've got an enormous mess on the countertop, and they won't stop pouring. The excess water doesn't quench your thirst any more than simply filling the glass did. If anything, the excess water beyond what you need only starts to cause you more problems, i.e., a puddle of water to clean up.

You need a glass of water to sate your thirst. Anything beyond this is want—and want adds nothing more that need didn't already give you.

What do you want in life, and what do you need? How much of your anxiety comes from your wants and not from your needs?

Ride the Wave

When you're confronted with irresistible cravings for things that aren't truly necessary, it also becomes crucial to recall Gandhi's timeless wisdom. His principle can be likened to navigating the formidable currents of the ocean. Resisting these cravings is like struggling against the relentless tides, an effort that can quickly deplete your energy. If you learn to ride these waves, however, you can skillfully navigate even the most turbulent seas.

Treat a craving like a wave, which builds in intensity before gradually receding. These waves represent the natural ebb and flow of our desires. Instead of engaging in a futile battle against them, adopt the role of a curious sailor, observing them with detached interest. When the urge for something unnecessary washes over you, ride it out without taking impulsive action. Keep in mind that cravings, much like waves, have a finite lifespan. They come, but they go again, and never last forever.

For instance, when that irresistible craving for potato chips strikes, acknowledge it as it surfaces. Recognize it for what it is—an artificial desire. Instead of immediately reaching for the chip bag, exercise patience. Redirect your focus to a different activity or take a few deep breaths. You'll notice that, like a wave cresting and then subsiding, the craving gradually dissipates.

As a teenager, I grappled with the relentless urge to seek comments on social media, i.e., I had a thirst for digital validation. I'd constantly check my phone, eagerly awaiting any updates. I began to see this behavior as a distraction, however, much like fleeting waves. Instead of immediately diving online, I learned to step back and redirect my focus to other meaningful activities. I'd watch the urge arise, then watch it fade again. It wasn't easy. But each time, it got a little easier. Over time, this shift allowed me to regain control, find tranquility, and prioritize my life choices beyond glowing screens.

Chapter 16: Cultivating Emotional Discernment

"Stoicism is about the domestication of emotions, not their elimination." —Nassim Nicholas Taleb

The Stoics get a bad name: Their philosophy isn't about putting your feelings in a dungeon somewhere and pretending they don't exist; it's more like turning them into valued houseguests. Instead of chasing your anger down the hallway with a broom, you're sipping tea together in the living room, discussing the matter like civilized adults.

So, in this journey of emotional domestication, we're armed with two powerful tools: emotional transmutation and emotional anticipation. These are like the handy gadgets in your emotional toolkit, helping you navigate the daily rollercoaster of life with a little more grace and humor and a lot less chaos. And it's *not* about emotional suppression.

Emotional Transmutation

All right, let's talk about emotional transmutation—it's like the alchemy of emotions. Imagine you're stuck in traffic, late for a meeting, and your patience is slipping away faster than ice cream on a hot summer day. It's tempting to honk your frustration at the poor car in front of you. But hold on, there's a Stoic trick here.

Instead of turning into a horn-honking banshee, consider the root of your anger. It might not be the traffic itself; it's more likely the fact that you're now the "fashionably late" guy. So, here's where emotional transmutation swoops in. You take a deep breath, and instead of erupting, you channel that anger into something productive. Maybe you strategize how to make up for lost time or ponder over ways to make your daily commute less soul-crushing.

Emotional transmutation is not about stuffing your feelings into a tiny emotional box; it's about getting creative with them. In our traffic jam scenario, it's turning road rage into a brainstorming session. The result? You not only cool the immediate emotional crisis but also start setting the stage for better solutions down the road (pun intended).

One of the great things about this practice is that it makes you the boss of your own emotions. You're not at the mercy of anger, sadness, or frustration. You're the one pulling their strings; they're not pulling yours. This newfound control allows you to face life's curveballs with a calm, strategic demeanor, which, spoiler alert, often leads to better outcomes.

Emotional Anticipation

Now let's dive into the second Stoic gem: anticipating your emotional reactions. Just think of it as emotional rehearsal, a mental dress rehearsal for life's unexpected dramas. It's like buying emotional insurance before the storm hits, and it's got a way of making you more present and far less anxious.

Stoicism suggests that we imagine the worst-case scenarios, the kind that would make a Shakespearean tragedy look like a walk in the park. It's not about becoming a doomsday prophet; it's about mental preparedness. When you anticipate the emotional rollercoaster that might come with life's curveballs, you're not blindsided by it. You're ready.

Let's say you're about to give a big presentation at work. Instead of imagining everyone in the room as potential tomato throwers, you imagine the projector going haywire, your tongue tying itself into knots, and the audience gazing at you like you just spoke in Klingon. This exercise isn't about self-torment; it's about being mentally and emotionally equipped to handle whatever happens. You've got contingency plans for emotional tornadoes.

Now, here's where the magic happens. By mentally rehearsing these worst-case scenarios, you become more present in the moment. Anxiety and overthinking take a back seat because, well, you've already seen the worst. You're not sweating the small stuff; you're ready for the big stuff. It's like going into a sword fight with armor while everyone else is wearing flip-flops.

This practice isn't about dwelling on negativity; it's about turning on the lights in the darkest corners of your mind. You're not paralyzed by fear; you're energized by preparedness. You become the superhero of your own emotional movie, calmly navigating the plot twists like a pro.

Anticipating your emotional reactions is like having a cheat code for life's challenges. It makes you more resilient, less anxious, and gives overthinking a run for its money. So, the next time life throws you a curveball, channel your inner Stoic and run through the worst-case scenarios. You'll be surprised how much smoother the ride becomes when you're mentally and emotionally equipped for the journey.

Chapter 17: Remember, YOU'RE the Master

"What worries you, masters you. —John Locke

Knowing Your Worry

In the twisted corridors of our minds, worries often lurk incognito, playing puppet master with our emotions. In the moment, we can fuse with these thoughts and ideas and forget that we're even having them. Perhaps by worrying, we feel as if we have some rudimentary control over a scary situation. But the truth is, worry is usually less our servant and more our master—every minute we spend worrying is a minute we spend in the clutches of a passive, impotent, irrational, and ineffective mindset (not to mention, it just feels awful, right?). The more we worry, the less able we are to solve problems, think creatively, enjoy ourselves, or notice opportunities.

Imagine having to summon the courage for a heart-to-heart chat with a close friend about a sensitive issue. It's the kind of situation that has your stomach doing gymnastics. Instead of churning over all the details and possible outcomes (i.e., getting trapped in your worry), take a moment to just admit, "Hey, I'm kind of freaked out about this talk." Consider it a friendly wave to your own anxiety. Suddenly, it's not the be-all and end-all. It's just something that's currently in your awareness.

Once you've given your worry a nod of recognition, the next act is vital: Shift your mental spotlight elsewhere. Dwelling on your worries is like binge-watching a never-ending reality show; there's no "next episode" button. You just automatically loop over to the next episode, and the next, and the next. Instead, consciously switch to a mental channel that brings you a sense of calm control.

In the context of that nerve-racking conversation, having acknowledged your worry, decide to switch gears. Make yourself a cup of tea, dive into a good book, or immerse yourself in that quirky hobby of yours.

Can you do anything about the situation?
If yes, then do it.
If no, then forcefully put your mind on something else that is useful or enjoyable.

If you catch your mind wandering to the conversation, double-check if this worry can be useful to you at all. "Hey, am I forgetting to plan something? Is there something I'm missing here?" Answer these questions for yourself, then move on. If you are truly prepared for the conversation and know what you want and need to say, for example, then imagine yourself literally thanking your brain, but also telling it that you no longer need its "help" and that you can handle things from here.

This perspective means that you are always converting worry into something more useful—either you are turning it into coping, accepting, and problem-solving, or you're using it to remind yourself to do something better with your time.

Worrying Isn't Just About Thinking

Let's move on to another tip: Worrying, as it turns out, is not a solo act confined to the mind. Instead, it's an intricate dance involving the mind, body, and life itself. Based on John Locke's wisdom, we can say that worrying isn't just about thinking. It's not merely a mental exercise; it's a full-fledged performance that shapes your actions, behaviors, and ultimately, your life's storyline. Your thoughts affect your feelings and your actions, and both of these influence the world you live in as well as the way you experience being in that world.

Do you want your worry to be the director of your play, orchestrating each scene? Do you want fear and rumination to always play the starring role? Every anxious thought plants a seed that can sprout into action, behavior, and ultimately, the path your life follows. It's a bit like writing a script for a drama; what you put on paper becomes the performance you live.

Fortunately, you're not condemned to watch this anxiety-driven production from the audience forever. You can take the reins, cut it off at the head, and change the script. It's all part of the grand theme of being more present and less anxious, of overthinking less, and of living a life unburdened by the weight of unnecessary worry.

Being present is your secret weapon in the battle against excessive worry. When you're fully engaged in the here and now, you're less likely to get entangled in the web of overthinking and anxiety about the future. It's like unplugging from the worry machine and plugging into the richness of the present moment. Being present might mean taking concrete action to help yourself, or it might mean gracefully accepting what's real without judgment and resistance. Either way, it's reality you're engaging with—not the nonsense in your mind.

Consider it as turning off the "what-if" projector that endlessly loops in your mind. Instead, you immerse yourself in the current scene, savoring the sights, sounds, and sensations of the present. This deliberate choice shifts your focus from an uncertain future to a tangible present, where you have more control and clarity.

Here's an analogy that can help you start treating your mind as a servant, not a master. Picture your life as a car traveling toward a destination. Many passengers are in the car, but only one driver. Each of us experiences doubt, anxiety, and fear—but do we want these experiences to be passengers or drivers? We don't have to be completely perfect and fearless—we just have to choose not to let our fear drive us... literally. Look your anxiety in the eyes and tell it, "I see you. I accept that you're here. But that doesn't mean you're in charge or that you get to drive this car. That's *my* job."

Chapter 18: Feel the Fear and Do It Anyway

"Serenity is knowing that your worst shot is still pretty good." —Johnny Miller

Our brains can sometimes be drama queens. We tend to go all Hollywood and imagine the worst possible scenarios, complete with total Armageddon and multiple feature-length disasters. For example, you've entered a competition, and in the leadup, you're so nervous and stressed out that you start conjuring up all kinds of fatal outcomes, ones where you not only lose the competition, but are completely mocked and denounced by the judges, thrown out of the event entirely, and prevented from ever attempting that activity ever again. You imagine crowds of people pointing and laughing (or booing? Or both?), and your tendency to ask, "What if . . ." starts to culminate in some, shall we say, *creative* thinking.

Welcome to the world of catastrophizing. It's easy to recognize when someone else is doing it—but when we do it, it can feel deadly serious.

Say No to Thinking the Worst

One of the essential keys to finding peace in the midst of uncertainty is to avoid catastrophizing. In reality, life rarely plays out like a blockbuster disaster movie. That's the first thing to understand. Even if things don't go according to plan, even if you stumble, or even if you face a catastrophe, it's unlikely to be as disastrous as your mind might make it seem. The world won't crumble, and the sky won't fall. Even if you do trip and fall, you sometimes tend to forget that you invariably get up again afterward, and life goes on. This understanding is the first step toward finding peace amid uncertainty.

Let me share a personal story as a writer. There have been countless moments in my writing journey when I've feared the worst. What if my ideas aren't good enough? What if people hate my work? What if I fail miserably? Catastrophic scenarios danced through my mind like overzealous actors on a Shakespearean stage. But when I pushed through those fears and wrote, even on my worst days, the outcomes weren't as catastrophic as my imagination had conjured.

For instance, there was a time when I was stuck with writer's block, and every word I typed seemed like a disaster in the making. I worried that my writing was terrible and that I'd never get published. But I decided to keep writing anyway, even if it was poorly crafted. To my surprise, some of those rough drafts eventually turned into pieces I was proud of, and they found their way into the hands of readers who appreciated them. The catastrophic scenarios in my mind were far more dramatic than the reality I faced.

The funny thing is, minor catastrophes did happen—and they still do. But by not endlessly stressing about them, I was actually able to face them, cope, take action where I could, and move on. This is the lie that catastrophizing tells you (actually, it's two lies): that something utterly catastrophic is going to happen, and that you won't be able to cope.

Real life can get gnarly, but usually, even on bad days, it's never one hundred percent totally and permanently terrible. If it's bad, it usually eases up after a while. If something goes wrong, there are usually a few things that went right. If you fail, there's often a lesson and a way forward. So, the first part is not true: Total catastrophe almost never happens. The second part is also not true: If bad things happen, you *can* cope. You can move on. You can even learn to go on and be better.

The lesson here is that it's better to attempt things, even if you do them poorly, than not do them at all, especially if they hold importance to you. Avoid the temptation to catastrophize, and you'll find that the peace you seek can often be found on the other side of your fears and doubts.

Embracing Effort

Johnny Miller's quote encourages us to shift our attention away from obsessing over potential negative outcomes and instead embrace the act of trying itself. It invites us to celebrate and acknowledge the effort we put into our endeavors, regardless of the immediate results.

Rather than losing sleep over what might go wrong or how our efforts might fall short, we should find solace in the mere fact that we tried. We took action—that's valuable no matter what the outcome is. This shift in perspective can help us be more present, reduce anxiety, and alleviate the tendency to overthink.

Now, let's explore this through the lens of my father's life as a writer. He's definitely my inspiration and also a perfect example of someone who truly embodied the notion of focusing on effort rather than fixating on outcomes. As a young writer, he had dreams of becoming a bestselling author, but the road to literary success was riddled with rejections and setbacks.

Instead of letting these challenges deter him, he chose to celebrate the simple act of writing every day. He understood that, regardless of whether his words found their way onto the bestseller list or not, the very act of pouring his thoughts onto paper was an achievement in itself. He was disciplined, and he worked hard. That was valuable in itself, and still is. This mindset not only reduced the pressure he placed on himself but also made his writing journey immensely enjoyable.

Over the years, my father's persistence and commitment to the craft paid off. He did have his share of successes, but more importantly, he found a deep sense of fulfillment in the process. He never looked back and regretted not writing more. He never let fears and anxieties get the better of him. It was as if he had discovered a treasure trove of serenity, knowing that, indeed, even his "worst shot" was still pretty good because it was a reflection of his dedication and passion.

This perspective, grounded in celebrating effort, not only made him a more prolific and confident writer but also a happier and less anxious individual. It serves as a powerful reminder that in our pursuit of peace and fulfillment, it's often the journey and the effort we invest that matter most, rather than the immediate outcomes we so often fixate upon. So, as we navigate life's uncertainties, let us remember to celebrate the act of trying and cherish the growth it brings, allowing us to be more present and less burdened by unnecessary anxiety and overthinking. This is a doorway into serenity that we can walk through even in the midst of catastrophe!

Chapter 19: It All Happens Here, in the Present

"No amount of anxiety can change the future. No amount of regret can change the past." —Karen Salmansohn

Ah, the future—that tantalizing, nebulous land of possibilities and uncertainties. It's natural for our minds to venture into its treacherous terrain, conjuring scenarios that range from utopian dreams to dystopian nightmares. It's a place where everything, anything can happen. Where maybe we'll be different—maybe better? Maybe worse?—and where all our dreams might come true or die once and for all.

But really, the future is . . . well, nothing. It's not real. It hasn't happened yet.

It is impossible to live the future in the present. All we can do is use language to talk *about* the future. But this is as useful as trying to eat the word "food." This is worth emphasizing—there actually is no way to "think about the future." All you can really do is hypnotize yourself with words right here and now in the present. And then, the future will arrive and be whatever it was going to be . . . but by the point where you are able to engage with it, it will simply be the present.

Anxiety Can't Change the Future

Let's dive deeper. Inspired by Salmansohn's wisdom, we need to recognize that excessive anxiety about the future does not have the power to change it. It's a bit like sitting in a rocking chair, constantly moving but never getting anywhere. Worrying about what's to come may give the illusion of control, but in reality, it's a futile exercise. The future unfolds on its own accord, regardless of our fretting and handwringing.

Now, let's put this into practical terms. When you're facing a major life decision, like changing careers, you may be haunted by thoughts of potential failure, financial instability, and what-ifs that keep you up at night. Here's the kicker: The more you dwell on these anxieties, the less equipped you are to make a well-informed decision. Why? Because instead of using your here-and-now present moment to do things like problem-solving or planning, you used it to hypnotize yourself with words about things that don't actually exist. Anxiety can be a black hole, consuming your mental bandwidth and leaving you paralyzed.

Let's imagine a scenario. Meet Alana, a dedicated professional who constantly worries about her work presentations. She envisions worst-case scenarios: stuttering through her slides, awkward silences, and disinterested stares from her colleagues. Actually, worse than that: she pictures wetting herself, passing out, slipping and falling in front of everyone . . . Each night, her anxiety takes her on a rollercoaster ride of fear and self-doubt. But here's the thing—all that anxiety won't magically transform her into a presentation wizard. It won't do a single thing but make her feel bad.

Recognizing this truth is the first step to change. Instead of letting anxiety consume her, Alana can choose to redirect her energy. She can focus on taking productive actions in the present, like researching her topic thoroughly, rehearsing her presentation, and seeking feedback from trusted colleagues. By channeling her energy into concrete steps, she not only improves her chances of success but also regains a sense of control over her situation.

Consider anxiety about the future as a leaky faucet. You can keep stressing about the dripping water, but until you pick up a wrench and fix it, the issue won't go away. By focusing on the actionable steps she can take in the present, Alana not only improves her presentation skills but also learns a valuable lesson about managing her anxiety.

It's about recognizing that you can't control the winds of the future, but you can adjust your sails. By taking action in the present, you shape your path forward. So, whether it's a career change, a personal relationship, or a big life decision, remember that anxiety alone won't navigate your ship.

Releasing Yourself from Past Regrets

Next, by the same token, understand that dwelling on past regrets cannot alter what has already occurred. It's like trying to unscramble an egg; once it's done, it's done. The past is a realm where we're mere spectators, not directors. Yet, many of us find ourselves lost in the labyrinth of "what if" and "if only" when it comes to our past decisions, as if our thoughts could build a time machine. We spend so much time crying over the milk already spilt that we forget about the milk we have right under our noses, or that we can simply go to the store and buy some more.

But as Salmansohn wisely points out, regrets are not a time machine; they're more like signposts. Instead of being trapped by them, we can use them as valuable lessons for personal growth. Imagine this: You regret not pursuing a degree in a field you were passionate about when you had the chance. You can't turn back the clock, but you can certainly course-correct in the present. There's an old idiom that says, "The best time to plant a tree was twenty years ago. The second-best time is today." That is true for everything. "I can't do the course at my age; I'll be fifty when I graduate!"—that's true. But then again, you'll be fifty anyway, so why not be fifty and have the qualification?

Let's paint a vivid picture to illustrate this point. Meet Mitchell, a middle-aged man who constantly broods over a failed business venture he attempted in his youth. Every day, he replays the scenes of financial hardship, missed opportunities, and the bitter taste of defeat. His regrets cast a long shadow over his life, making him feel like a prisoner in his own past.

Now, here's where the magic happens. Mitchell decides to heed Salmansohn's wisdom and transform his regrets into lessons for personal growth. Instead of wallowing in self-pity, he starts to dissect the mistakes he made during that business venture. He identifies the key lessons: the importance of thorough market research, the need for a solid business plan, and the value of perseverance in the face of setbacks. Every mistake is transformed into a valuable, usable lesson.

Mitchell's newfound perspective on his past empowers him to make wiser choices in the present. He starts a new business with a well-researched plan, a mentor to guide him, and the determination to learn from his past missteps. As he does so, the weight of his past regrets gradually lifts, and he becomes more present in his endeavors.

Regret, when used as a teacher rather than a tormentor, can be a catalyst for personal growth. It's like turning a compass that once pointed backward into one that guides you forward. By recognizing that the past is unchangeable and focusing on the lessons it offers, you free yourself from the chains of regret and become more present in your own life.

It's about letting go of the anchors of the past that weigh you down and embracing the sails of growth in the present. By applying this mindset shift to various aspects of your life, you not only become more present but also less anxious and less prone to overthinking. Regrets lose their power when they become steppingstones on your journey rather than stumbling blocks.

Chapter 20: Just Breathe

"[Slow breathing] is like an anchor in the midst of an emotional storm: The anchor won't make the storm go away, but it will hold you steady until it passes." — Russ Harris

Isn't it amusing how life can be so changeable, with its constant waves of unpredictability and those sudden emotional squalls? Think about the things that you were terrified of ten or twenty years ago. Things don't quite look the same anymore, do they? Like waking up to a beautiful calm morning, it's hard to remember the violent storm of the night before. Your emotional weather always changes, and what seemed at age fifteen like the worst thing in the world barely makes a blip when you are thirty-five years old. Just as any seasoned sailor worth their weight in sea salt will insist, the secret to staying afloat in bad weather lies in having a reliable anchor.

Grounding Yourself with Slow-Breathing Techniques

First, when facing an emotional storm, employ slow-breathing techniques as a powerful tool to ground yourself. Slow, deliberate breaths act as an anchor, helping you maintain stability and composure amidst turbulent emotions.

Slow breathing serves as a lifebuoy for the turbulent waters of emotions. It's a simple yet remarkably effective technique to regain your footing when you feel like you're being tossed about by the storm. I remember a particularly stressful day at work, where deadlines seemed to multiply like rabbits, and I was on the verge of losing my cool. It was during such a tempest that I discovered the magic of slow breathing.

As my stress levels soared that day, I retreated to a quiet corner, determined to regain my composure. With each inhale and exhale, I consciously slowed down my breathing. Deep breath in, counting to four. Slow breath out, counting to six. Inhale. Exhale. Repeat. It felt like I was dropping an anchor in the chaotic sea of my thoughts. Gradually, the storm within me began to subside. The tight knot of anxiety loosened, and a sense of calm washed over me.

That experience was a revelation. I realized that slow breathing wasn't just a theoretical concept but a tangible lifeline in the tumultuous sea of emotions. By deliberately controlling my breath, I could exert control over my emotional state. It was as if I had discovered a secret superpower that allowed me to stay grounded when life's waves threatened to capsize me.

Slow breathing became my go-to tool in times of emotional upheaval. Whether dealing with personal challenges, conflicts, or even moments of overwhelming joy, I harnessed this technique to navigate the emotional rollercoaster of life. It's like having a trusty anchor that I could drop whenever I needed to stabilize myself in the turbulent waters of existence.

Embracing the Temporary Nature of Emotions

Next, understand that emotions, like storms, are temporary. No matter how bad they are, they pass. Always. Instead of resisting or trying to force them away, acknowledge and accept them as a natural part of the human experience. You don't have to resist them or solve them or fight against them—just ride them out and remember that you are not the storm.

This profound wisdom about emotions being temporary, much like passing storms, has been a game changer in my quest to be more present and less anxious. It's a lesson I learned during a hiking adventure in the wilderness, an experience that unfolded like a metaphor for life itself.

As I embarked on a challenging mountain hike, a sense of excitement and trepidation filled me. The trail was breathtaking, with lush forests, cascading waterfalls, and panoramic vistas. However, as the hours passed and fatigue set in, anxiety and self-doubt began to creep in. My inner voice was quick to point out how far I had to go, how tired I felt, and whether I could even make it to the summit.

That's when I remembered the advice about emotions being like storms. Instead of resisting these feelings of anxiety and self-doubt, I chose to acknowledge them as natural responses to a demanding situation. I told myself that it was okay to feel this way, that these emotions were just passing clouds in the sky of my mind.

As I continued to climb, I noticed something remarkable happening. The more I accepted my feelings, the less power they had over me. It was as though I had surrendered to the storm and, in doing so, found a sense of peace amidst the chaos. I began to appreciate the beauty of the journey, even in moments of discomfort.

This lesson extended beyond the hike itself. I realized that in daily life, I often resisted negative emotions, trying to push them away or berating myself for feeling them. This resistance only fueled my anxiety and overthinking. However, by adopting the perspective that emotions, like storms, are temporary and natural, I found a way to be more present in my life. Think of it this way—you could fiercely try to stand firm against a storm and use all your might to push against the strong waves. Or, you could learn to ride on top of the waves and *surf* them.

Instead of constantly worrying about the future or ruminating over the past, I began to focus on the present moment. I learned to embrace my emotions, whether they were joyous or challenging, as part of the rich tapestry of human experience. This shift in perspective reduced my anxiety and allowed me to overthink less. It was like finding a calm center amidst life's storms.

Chapter 21: Worry ... But Do It on Your Terms

Let's take a look at an enlightening study by Annika Dippel, Jos F. Brosschot, and Bart Verkuil that offers us valuable insights into the art of worry management.

The researchers delved into eight different studies, encompassing nearly a thousand participants, primarily female. What did they uncover? Well, they stumbled upon a fascinating strategy: worry postponement or stimulus control.

Now, why is this worth our attention? This discovery sheds light on a simple yet potent approach to combat anxiety effectively—establishing regular and consistent patterns in our daily lives. Let's explore this innovative approach to worry management together with two everyday strategies.

Managing Your Worry

First, develop worry awareness. It's like shining a light on the dark corners of your thoughts and becoming aware that you are, in fact, worrying. One effective way to do this is by keeping a worry log and then crafting a designated worry period. Let's delve into why this is important and how to make it work for you.

Often, anxiety lurks in the background of our minds, like a shadowy figure we can't quite see clearly. We feel it, and it influences us, but we're not really aware of this influence and where it's coming from. By keeping a worry log, you bring these worries into the light. You become more aware of the specific triggers, patterns, and times when anxiety tends to creep in.

Imagine you notice that most of your worries hit you like a tidal wave in the late afternoon or before bedtime. This is a valuable insight. It tells you that these are the moments when anxiety has a stronger grip on your thoughts. Armed with this knowledge, you can prepare to confront these worries head-on.

Once you've identified the times when you're most prone to worry, it's time to establish a worry period. This is a designated time, place, and duration where you allow yourself to worry. In fact, you deliberately *make* yourself worry during this time—how's that for being in control? The key here is that you're in charge of when and how you engage with your worries.

Choose a comfortable and quiet place for your worry period. Set a specific time, like 5 p.m., and allocate a fixed duration, say fifteen minutes. During this time, give yourself permission to worry as intensely as you want about anything and everything. It's your worry time, after all.

By isolating your worries to a particular time slot, you regain control over your thoughts. When worries pop up at other times, you can gently tell yourself, "Not now, I have my worry period later. Then I can worry as much as I like." This postponement reduces the impact of worries throughout the day, allowing you to focus on the present without being overwhelmed by anxiety.

Goal-Oriented Worry Reduction

Next, make it a goal to reduce worry rather than eliminate it entirely. Striving for perfection can be an undue burden when it comes to reducing anxiety and embracing a more present, less overthinking-prone life. Instead, setting achievable and measurable objectives can pave the way to a calmer state of mind. Let's explore this concept further.

Worry is a part of life, but it doesn't have to dominate your thoughts. Consider a goal like this: "I will spend ten minutes on worrying this week and only five minutes next week." This objective acknowledges that worry will still exist, but it's striving for a gradual reduction in the time and mental energy devoted to it. This makes the goal less daunting and more achievable.

Setting measurable goals for reducing worry ties into the broader theme of being more present. When you commit to spending less time worrying, you free up mental space to focus on the here and now. This shift in attention cultivates mindfulness, as you become more attuned to the present moment.

Another goal could be: "I will avoid what triggers my worry for ten minutes." This encourages you to deliberately steer your thoughts away from worry triggers, even if just for a short time. It's a step toward greater mindfulness, as you redirect your attention to the present rather than ruminating on future concerns. When you've achieved it, you'll feel more able to shift the goal posts to fifteen minutes, and so on.

Achieving these realistic goals provides a sense of accomplishment. Celebrate each milestone, whether it's reducing your worry time or successfully redirecting your thoughts from triggers. These victories reinforce your ability to manage worry, gradually making it a less dominant force in your life.

Making it a goal to reduce worry rather than eliminate it acknowledges the imperfection of progress. It empowers you to set achievable and measurable objectives, fostering a more present and less anxious mindset. By gradually reducing the time and mental space you allocate to worry, you embark on a mindful journey toward a calmer, more balanced life. So, set those realistic goals, measure your progress, and relish in the growing moments of peace and presence in your life.

Chapter 22: Find Relief in Ritual

According to a study conducted by researchers from Tel Aviv University, the key to reducing anxiety may be found in recognizing the significance of establishing consistent and regular patterns in our daily routines.

At first glance, the idea might appear counterintuitive. How can something as commonplace as adhering to a routine contribute to anxiety alleviation? The answer, intriguingly, is rooted in our fundamental human need for structure and predictability. We flourish when there's a sense of order in our lives, when we can anticipate what lies ahead.

Routines, in this regard, provide us with the vital framework we crave. They act as guiding beacons, diminishing the haze of ambiguity and unpredictability that often fuels our anxiety. Now, based on this study, let's explore two tips that can help you find relief in routines.

Embracing Consistency for Anxiety Reduction

One tip is to recognize the immense value of establishing regular and consistent patterns in your daily life. These patterns, also known as simply having routines, extend their calming influence to various aspects of our lives, including waking up and going to bed, meal times, exercise, and leisure activities.

Imagine the act of waking up in the morning without a set routine. Each day, you wake up at a different time, unsure of what awaits you. The lack of structure can lead to a sense of disorientation and increased anxiety. Now, consider an alternative scenario: You establish a consistent wake-up time and a series of morning rituals.

Perhaps you start your day with some light stretching or enjoy a cup of herbal tea. This routine becomes a reliable anchor. It communicates to your brain that the day is starting as planned, offering a sense of control and predictability. Over time, this simple morning ritual can significantly reduce morning anxiety and set a positive tone for the day ahead.

Consistent mealtime routines can also wield a powerful influence. In a hectic life, meals are often rushed or skipped entirely. This erratic eating pattern can trigger physical and emotional stress. However, by carving out specific times for meals and adhering to them consistently, you create a structured, nourishing experience. Picture sitting down at the same time each day to savor your lunch, free from distractions, and relishing the flavors and textures of your food. This not only promotes healthier eating habits but also provides a tranquil pause in your day, reducing overall anxiety.

Exercise is another area where routines can make a substantial impact on anxiety reduction. Irregular workout schedules can lead to feelings of guilt or frustration when you miss a session. However, when you establish a consistent exercise routine, whether it's a morning jog, yoga class, or evening weightlifting session, you build discipline and structure into your life. The predictability of knowing when and how you'll engage in physical activity can alleviate anxiety, boost motivation, and improve your overall sense of well-being.

Even leisure activities can benefit from routine. While relaxation and spontaneity are essential, setting aside dedicated times for hobbies and downtime can help you unwind more effectively. Whether it's reading a book, painting, or practicing a musical instrument, having designated periods for these activities ensures they become integral parts of your life. This balance between structure and leisure can be a soothing balm for anxiety, offering moments of solace and rejuvenation in an otherwise bustling routine.

Recognizing the value of establishing regular and consistent patterns in your daily life is a potent strategy for reducing anxiety. Through structured routines in activities like waking up and going to bed, mealtimes, exercise, and leisure pursuits, you can regain a sense of control, predictability, and balance in your life. These routines become your allies, grounding you amidst the chaos of modern living and empowering you to navigate each day with greater ease and peace of mind.

Seeking Solace in Repetition

Another powerful strategy is to find comfort in repetition. Engaging in activities that involve repetition can be a source of solace and mindfulness, allowing you to be fully immersed in the moment and reduce overthinking.

Repetition can take many forms in our lives, from simple daily rituals to more intricate hobbies and practices. The essence of finding comfort in repetition lies in the soothing rhythm and familiarity that it provides. When you engage in repetitive activities, your mind becomes less preoccupied with worries about the past or the future. Instead, you are drawn into the present moment, allowing you to savor each experience fully.

Consider the act of knitting, a classic example of finding comfort in repetition. The rhythmic motion of the needles, the familiar click-clack sound they make, and the gradual formation of a fabric create a meditative experience. As you knit, you are wholly absorbed in the tactile sensation of the yarn, the gentle swaying of your hands, and the progression of your work. In this process, you relinquish the burden of overthinking, finding solace in the repetitive nature of the craft.

Finding comfort in repetition extends to everyday rituals, such as cooking or gardening. These activities involve a series of repeated motions and steps. Chopping vegetables or tending to plants can be therapeutic as you immerse yourself in the tactile sensations and sensory experiences they offer. You find peace in the predictability of the process, leaving little room for anxiety to take hold.

Chapter 23: Two Stressed People Means Less Stress

Does this scenario sound a bit familiar? You're about to give a high-stress presentation. Your heart is racing, your palms are sweaty, and your mind is racing with anxious thoughts. It feels like the world's weight is on your shoulders, and stress and anxiety are taking hold, right?

A study led by Sarah Townsend, a professor at USC Marshall School of Business, shows that these moments of high stress are pretty common. In the moment, it might feel as though you are all alone in battling your demons, but the truth is that anxiety and stress happen to everyone—and bearing this in mind can actually help you cope.

Townsend studied how people deal with their emotions during stressful situations. She had fifty-two female students talk about their feelings before giving speeches, and what she found has important lessons for handling stress and being more resilient.

Here's the deal: If you talk about your feelings with someone who feels the same way, it can help you feel less stressed. Imagine you're both in a boat, and you're both in rough waters. When you talk to each other about how scary it is, you're no longer on your own, but rowing together. This perception of teamwork reduces stress.

Finding Emotional Support

When the going gets tough, one of the most effective strategies for managing stress is to seek emotional support from colleagues or friends who share a similar emotional profile when facing daunting situations. This support can act as a potent stress-relief mechanism by providing a sense of camaraderie and shared experience.

Let's say you're part of a tight-knit project team tasked with a critical presentation to top-tier clients. As the presentation date looms closer, your anxiety levels soar. In this moment, you decide to reach out to a colleague who has been in similar high-pressure situations before. You share your concerns, and to your surprise, they nod in understanding, recounting their own experiences of sweaty palms and racing hearts.

By connecting this way, you not only feel seen and heard, but you have real-world proof that others can survive what you are currently battling. This shared emotional experience helps normalize your own emotions and reduces feelings of isolation. Together, you might even devise strategies to prepare for the presentation, such as practicing, time management, and relaxation techniques.

This may explain how someone who experiences a severe personal challenge (like divorce or violence) on their own may develop PTSD, whereas people who collectively experience a disaster (like a flood or earthquake) tend to fair much better. There's strength in numbers, and in a shared experience! That said, this isn't license to look for a fellow catastrophizer—it's an important distinction to beware of.

Enhancing Emotional Connection through Active Listening

Another valuable tool is practicing active listening when someone shares their feelings with you. Active listening involves not just hearing the words but making a genuine effort to understand and empathize with the emotions behind those words, while refraining from interrupting or judging. By doing so, you not only validate their feelings but also encourage them to delve deeper into their emotions, promoting a sense of trust and empathy. In return, this fosters emotional resonance between you and the speaker. And while all this is going on, you're not anxiously ruminating and overthinking.

Imagine a scenario where your close friend Emily confides in you about her recent struggles at work. She's clearly stressed and anxious about a challenging project, and you notice her demeanor reflecting the weight of her emotions. Instead of immediately offering advice or attempting to "fix" her situation, you practice active listening.

You sit down with Emily, maintain eye contact, and nod to show you're engaged. You resist the urge to interject with your own stories or solutions. Instead, you gently ask open-ended questions like "Tell me more about what's been going on" or "How do you feel about this situation?" Your genuine interest encourages Emily to share her feelings more deeply.

As Emily continues to speak, you find yourself genuinely connecting with her emotions. You empathize with her stress, acknowledging that her concerns are valid. By the end of your conversation, Emily not only feels heard and understood, but the act of sharing has also eased her anxiety. Even better, you notice that you yourself feel less stressed—and have a far more balanced perspective on all the things that are currently worrying you.

The central theme here is that in our fast-paced world filled with distractions, the art of active listening can be a powerful antidote to anxiety and overthinking. It reminds us that by offering our full presence, empathetic ear, and understanding, we can not only provide solace to others but also find a profound sense of presence and perspective within ourselves.

Chapter 24: "And What Does that Mean . . . ?"

Let's break down a fascinating study here brought to you by Lisa Vittorio and colleagues on the role of Socratic questioning in CBT—a powerful weapon against anxious overthinking and depression. The researchers recruited 123 therapy-goers and examined the way they responded to different kinds of questions.

Here's what they found: Socratic questioning was extremely effective at helping change people's ingrained thought patterns. Named after the philosopher who was notorious for feigning ignorance in order to lead debate and dialogue, Socratic questions are all about using inquiry to uncover hidden assumptions. Rather than taking anything at face value, a Socratic question makes inquiries about those very things we take to be true but haven't properly examined. One of the greatest Socratic/CBT-style questions is merely to ask: *do you have any evidence for that belief?*

Similarly, Socratic questions can help us arrive at underlying core beliefs by challenging our assumptions. If, for example, we keep asking, "And what does that mean?" we tend to arrive at certain key schemas and thought patterns that are influencing our lives. For example:

I'm going to make a mess of my new business.
If you did mess it up, what would that mean?
Well, obviously it would mean I'd burn through my savings and fail to make a profit.
And so? What would that mean?
It would mean I'd be broke.
What's so bad about that?
Well . . . then everyone would think I'm an awful loser.
If they did think you were an awful loser . . . what would that mean?
It would mean that I'm a bad person.

Here, with just a few well-placed Socratic questions, we uncover the deeper fear, and the belief that comes with it, i.e., "If I fail at this business, it will mean I'm a bad person."

We can even continue with more Socratic questioning—for example, do you have any evidence for that belief? Is that really true?

Challenging Negative Thought Patterns

Imagine this scenario: You've had a rough day at work, and you're sitting in traffic, stewing in frustration. Negative thoughts creep in, like "I'm always stuck in traffic" or "My boss is out to get me." Now, instead of letting those thoughts spiral out of control, you can use the technique of questioning.

When you notice these thoughts, hit the mental pause button. Don't let them run rampant. Ask yourself, "What evidence do I have for this thought?" In the traffic scenario, you might realize that you're not *always* stuck; it's just been a few bad days. And as for your boss, well, maybe there's no concrete evidence to support that suspicion.

Dig deeper by asking, "Is there an alternative explanation?" Maybe the traffic snarl is due to an accident or roadwork. As for your boss, could their behavior be a result of stress or personal issues? Exploring alternative explanations can dial down the negativity.

Here's where you enlist your inner Sherlock Holmes. Ask, "What would a close friend say about this situation?" Think about what advice you'd offer if your friend was in your shoes. Chances are, you'd be more compassionate and rational with them. Applying this perspective can help you gain insight into your own thoughts and emotions.

By practicing the power of questioning, you're essentially becoming your own cognitive therapist. You're challenging and reframing those negative thought patterns. It's like swapping out a distorted fun house mirror for what accurately reflects reality. Over time, this practice can lead to a more positive and balanced mindset, even when you're stuck in traffic or dealing with stress.

Chapter 25: You Need to Unplug

Are you ever been struck by the feeling that your life in the digital age resembles an overstuffed closet? We're constantly accumulating, storing, and sifting through a vast repository of information at our fingertips. Yet, amid this endless digital cacophony, the more we gather, the less we seem to find. It's as if we're navigating through a maze of distractions, struggling to focus on what truly matters. It's the modern world's paradox: As we gain more access to information, we often lose touch with ourselves.

In a fascinating study led by Jeffrey Lambert, PhD, the research team set out to explore the impact of a one-week break from social media platforms like Facebook, Twitter, Instagram, and TikTok. They enrolled 154 participants, averaging 29.6 years in age, in a randomized controlled trial. What they uncovered was nothing short of astonishing—those who abstained from social media for the week experienced significant improvements in well-being, reductions in depression, and lessened anxiety. These findings shine a light on the potential benefits of short-term social media breaks—and hint at the potential power of longer-term interventions.

Reclaiming Mental Space with a Social Media Detox

If you'd like to take a stand against digital distraction, the first thing to do is decide on a duration that suits your lifestyle and goals. This decision is crucial because it sets the tone for your digital sabbatical. It could be as short as a few days, giving you a brief but effective mental reset, or you might opt for a more extended break of a week or even a month. The key is to choose a time frame that feels achievable and realistic for you.

I have an admission to make: I used to be social-media obsessed. But back then, I'd felt increasingly overwhelmed. It felt like a never-ending stream of notifications, updates, and messages vying for my attention. I knew I needed a break, but the thought of completely disconnecting from my digital world was daunting. So, I decided to start with a one-week detox.

During that week, I discovered the true power of deliberate disconnection. Initially, it was challenging. The habit of reaching for my phone and mindlessly scrolling through my feeds was deeply ingrained. However, as the days passed, I noticed a significant shift in my mental state. The noise of social media gradually faded, and in its place, I found moments of clarity and calm.

I used the time I would have spent on social media to engage in activities that truly mattered to me. I read books I'd been meaning to get to, spent quality time with loved ones, and even started a new hobby. I felt more present in each moment, without the constant distraction of notifications pulling me away. By the end of the week, I realized that I had not only regained control over my mental well-being but also reconnected with the essence of my life. I decided that while I'd dabble here and there, in the future I wanted a much more mindful relationship with technology, and I would stay conscious of how it affected me day to day. The mindset changes from that week are still with me today.

A social media detox, regardless of its duration, can be a transformative experience. It offers a much-needed break from the relentless onslaught of information, allowing you to reset your mental state. And beyond this, it allows you to regain control, reconnect with your values, and consider if there are healthier ways to move forward.

Embracing Real-World Connections

While social media can help us stay connected, it often comes at the cost of genuine human contact. To enhance your overall well-being and reduce the negative impact of social media on your mental health, another tip is to shift your focus back to the tangible world around you. Yes, I want you to go out there!

One striking example of the power of face-to-face interactions comes from a friend of mine, Kayleigh. She had always been an avid social media user, constantly checking her accounts and feeling the pressure to curate a perfect online image. She noticed, however, that this constant digital presence was taking a toll on her mental health. She decided to make a change and started actively seeking more real-world connections. She began to prioritize in-person gatherings with friends and family, even scheduling regular coffee dates and game nights.

Over time, Kayleigh found that these face-to-face interactions not only reduced her anxiety but also helped her overthink less. When she was engaged in meaningful conversations or shared laughter with loved ones, her worries about her online persona seemed distant and insignificant. The genuine connections she fostered in the real world provided her with a sense of fulfillment and belonging that social media couldn't replicate.

She also started immersing herself in hobbies and passion projects. Many of us spend excessive amounts of time scrolling through our feeds, but what if we redirected that energy into something we're genuinely passionate about? Whether it's painting, playing a musical instrument, gardening, or any other hobby, these activities can help us be more present in the moment.

And that's not all! Spending time in nature is another powerful antidote to the digital noise that surrounds us. Nature has a remarkable ability to ground us and reduce anxiety. Whether it's a leisurely walk in the park, a hike in the mountains, or simply sitting by a serene lake, nature provides a respite from the constant demands of social media.

Fostering face-to-face interactions, engaging in hobbies, and spending time in nature are essential steps toward being more present in your life and reducing the negative impact of social media on your mental health. These real-world experiences allow you to escape the digital noise and anxiety, replacing them with genuine connections, passion, and a profound sense of tranquility.

Chapter 26: Stick to the Facts

"Never exaggerate. It is a matter of great importance to forego superlatives, in part to avoid offending the truth, and in part to avoid cheapening your judgment." —Baltasar Gracián

Our ancient ancestors developed physiological machinery to help them survive threat. They learned to recognize, for example, a dangerous tiger prowling in the forest. Modern man, however, has developed language, and this tool has an interesting property: It can evoke powerful physical and emotional states in us. In other words, we can *read words* describing a scary and threatening situation and reproduce in our bodies precisely the same fight-or-flight response as our ancestors did when they encountered the real tiger in the real forest. The unreal can create the real. Threatening words can create the perception of threat, which can become real for us.

When we think threatening thoughts, the same thing happens. It's just a quirk of the tool of language; one of the side effects of being able to conjure up hypothetical and non-real situations is that we are then also able to terrify ourselves! When we say, "Everything is doomed," we need to remember that we are, in a very real sense, listening to ourselves.

As we embark on our quest for serenity, we can find guidance in the wisdom of Baltasar Gracián, who cautioned against the perils of exaggeration and championed the deliberate and more limited use of language. Is everything doomed? Really? Or is your printer just broken? Words matter—especially if we are stressing ourselves out unnecessarily by using words in a sloppy way. Instead let's learn to wield words with precision and to start using them to control and manage our anxiety, rather than to fire it up.

Mindful Use of Superlatives

The way we use superlatives in our language can have a profound impact on our emotional well-being. Often, we might find ourselves prone to exaggerated statements that magnify our worries and anxieties. To effectively manage anxiety, let's talk about the first tip: Use superlatives mindfully. This means avoiding excessive or inappropriate usage and reserving them for situations or qualities that genuinely deserve such extreme descriptions.

Consider the following scenario: You're facing a challenging situation at work, and your initial reaction is to declare, "This is the worst situation ever!" While this may express your frustration, it can also intensify your anxiety. More than this, it can convince you that this emotional appraisal is an accurate reflection of reality itself. Though you might *feel* as though this is the worst situation, that doesn't follow that it truthfully is. Instead, try a more balanced description like, "This is a challenging situation." Can you feel the difference it makes to say this rather than make an exaggerated claim? By substituting "worst" with "challenging," you acknowledge the difficulty without catastrophizing it.

The essence of this tip lies in keeping your judgment realistic. Most problems or situations we encounter in life have realistic solutions, even if they appear complex at first. When you describe them accurately, you create a mental framework that allows you to see them as manageable challenges rather than insurmountable obstacles. This shift in perspective can significantly reduce anxiety and provide a clearer path for effective problem-solving.

To apply this principle in your own life, start by paying attention to your language. Notice when you catch yourself using superlatives like "worst," "best," "always," or "never." Take a moment to reflect on whether these extreme descriptors are genuinely warranted in the context. Are they helping you to cope, to solve the problem, or to feel better in any way? If not, consider a more measured and accurate way to express your thoughts.

For example, suppose you're dealing with a tight deadline for a project. Instead of saying, "I swear to God this deadline is going to kill me," acknowledge the pressure by saying, "This is a challenging deadline, but I can break it down into manageable tasks." By avoiding excessive superlatives and maintaining realistic judgments, you can keep your anxiety levels in check and approach difficulties with greater composure and confidence.

Using superlatives mindfully involves refraining from excessive or inappropriate usage and reserving them for truly exceptional situations. By applying this tactic, you can reduce anxiety and approach life's challenges with a more realistic and constructive mindset. Remember that most problems have solutions, and by using language judiciously, you empower yourself to navigate them effectively.

Practicing Emotional Moderation

The second tip involves a simple yet powerful technique: When you find yourself swept up by an extreme emotion, whether it's positive or negative, take a moment to measure its intensity on a scale from one to ten. If it registers as a ten, it's time to step back and refrain from making any significant decisions or judgments.

This approach recognizes that extreme emotions, whether joy or despair, can cloud our judgment and lead to impulsive reactions that we might later regret. By taking a step back when your emotions are at their peak, you allow yourself the space to observe the emotion as it runs its course. The goal is to wait until the emotional intensity subsides to around a five on the scale. At this point, your emotions are likely to be more manageable, and your decision-making will be clearer and less driven by the immediate emotional response.

This principle is rooted in the idea that maintaining an even keel emotionally can lead to a more present and less anxious existence. It helps you avoid overthinking and impulsive actions that often result from heightened emotions. Whether you're experiencing the thrill of success or the depths of disappointment, learning to be aware of and moderate your emotional responses can lead to a more balanced and mindful approach to life.

To practice this in your own life, start by cultivating awareness of your emotional responses. When you encounter a situation that triggers a strong emotion, pause for a moment. Ask yourself, "On a scale of one to ten, how intense is this emotion right now?" If it's a ten, remind yourself that it's time to step back and resist making any hasty decisions or judgments.

As you observe the emotion running its course, practice mindfulness. Focus on your breath and physical sensations to stay grounded in the present moment. This allows you to disengage from the immediate emotional turbulence and gain perspective. Once the emotion has naturally subsided to a five or lower, you can then approach the situation with a clearer mind and a reduced likelihood of overthinking or reacting impulsively.

Practicing emotional moderation aligns with the goal of being more present and less anxious. By measuring the intensity of your emotions and allowing them to subside before making decisions or judgments, you create a space for mindfulness and rational thinking.

A caveat, however: just because you are aware and taking an objective stance on your emotions, it doesn't mean that you are repressing or avoiding them. If you are afraid, acknowledge that. If you are ebullient and full of happiness, enjoy that feeling. The trick is to never lose sight of the fact that you are having a transient emotional experience. Whatever it is, it will pass, and while it's here, it doesn't have to define you.

Chapter 27: The Fastest Way to Find Perspective

"'Memento mori,' the monarch whispered. 'Remember death. Even for those who wield great power, life is brief. There is only one way to triumph over death, and that is by making our lives masterpieces.'" —Dan Brown

How often do you catch yourself lost in the labyrinth of your thoughts, overwhelmed by life's myriad choices and worries? It's an affliction that plagues many of us in the modern world, where the pace of life and the deluge of information can leave our minds in a state of perpetual turmoil. In such times, we could all use a compass to navigate the chaos and complexity. And this compass is none other than "memento mori," a phrase that has echoed through the ages, whispered by kings and scholars alike.

As the quote from Dan Brown suggests, "memento mori" invites us to remember death, to acknowledge the impermanence of life, and to embrace it as a guiding force in our decisions. It's as powerful a tool today as it was in ancient times.

Mindful Decision-Making with Memento Mori

The first tip on our list is a compass for navigating life's treacherous waters with style and grace. Imagine you're at a crossroads, a pivotal moment that could shape your destiny. Instead of feeling overwhelmed, you decide to pause and remember your mortality, "memento mori."

You stand there, poised and ready, and you ask yourself, "If time is a rare, precious commodity, how do I want to spend it? What truly sets my soul on fire? Who am I really, and what ought I to do with my time here on this earth?" These questions aren't here to spook or overwhelm you; rather they're here to cut through the noise and nonsense. They're a secret weapon for making wise, masterful decisions that resonate with you on a deeper level.

You have limited time on this earth; do you want to spend it arguing with strangers on a low-quality internet forum? One day, you will close your eyes and never open them again; do you want to waste your eyes right now, in this moment, watching reruns of a show you didn't even like the first time around?
One day soon, you will be old and looking back on your life; do you want to say that the height of your achievement was avoiding risk and responsibility?

Before I became a full-time author, I was ensnared in the corporate rat race, chasing promotions and paychecks like they were the holy grail. It was a frenzied existence, a never-ending quest for more without ever pausing to ponder if it was what I truly craved.

And then, in strides "memento mori." I decided to put it to the test. I mused, "If my days were numbered, what would I regret not having done?" The answers were crystal clear: quality time with family, personal growth, and forging bonds with fellow earthlings.

So, I did the unthinkable. I hit the reset button on my life. More family gatherings, more time to write, fewer late nights at the office. I enrolled in writing courses that fed my soul, and fostered relationships that enriched my spirit. And guess what? My career didn't nosedive into oblivion; it soared to new heights because I was now a laser-focused, passion-driven writer.

Making decisions with "memento mori" as my co-pilot wasn't scary at all; it was liberating. It stripped away the unnecessary and left me with a clear roadmap to what truly mattered. The noise of life may look complicated at times, but reminding yourself of what's ultimately important can simplify things right down again. So, the next time you find yourself at life's crossroads, don't sweat the choices. Embrace "memento mori" as your guiding star and let it lead you to a life that's more meaningful.

Applying Memento Mori to Anxious Thoughts

Memento mori isn't just about contemplating the finite nature of human life; it extends its wisdom to the anxious thoughts that often plague our minds. Picture this: You're lying awake at night, your thoughts spiraling into a whirlpool of worries and fears. Here's another tip—you can use the same "memento mori" principle to quell those anxious thoughts.

Whenever you find yourself engulfed by overthinking, take a moment to reflect. Remember that even your most negative thoughts have an expiration date. Just as everything in life is transient, so, too, are your worries and fears. They may feel overwhelming in the moment, but like clouds passing in the sky, they, too, shall pass.

Consider also that worry seldom achieves anything. Okay, not seldom—it *never* achieves anything. Wouldn't you rather use the time you do have to make changes and accept what can't be changed? It's like going to watch a play at a grand playhouse and spending the entire time at the door, ruminating over which seat you should pick. Every moment you spend doing that is a moment you're not spending actually enjoying the show.

I used to be a chronic overthinker. My mind had a knack for conjuring the most intricate scenarios of disaster and doom, and I was very good at believing every last detail. It was as if I had a mental treadmill, and I couldn't figure out how to turn it off.

That's when I decided to harness the power of "memento mori" for my anxious thoughts. When I caught myself spiraling into a vortex of worry, I paused and reminded myself that these thoughts, too, were fleeting. I visualized them as passing clouds, coming and going without leaving a lasting impact.

This simple practice began to transform my relationship with anxiety. It allowed me to step back and put things into perspective as I realized that most of my worries were based on scenarios that were unlikely to happen. I started to approach life with a more present mindset, focusing on the here and now rather than dwelling on an uncertain future.

Over time, the intensity of my anxious feelings began to wane. I learned to appreciate the beauty of being present in the moment, free from the shackles of overthinking. "Memento mori" had not only guided my decisions but also helped me find peace and clarity in the midst of life's chaos.

So, remember, just as life is impermanent, so are your worries. Embrace the idea that your anxious thoughts, too, shall pass. By doing so, you can navigate life with greater presence, less anxiety, and a newfound ability to conquer overthinking one fleeting thought at a time.

Chapter 28: What's Your Default State?

"Here's a suggestion: Find out how to make zero deeply satisfying. Then the rest just flows forward as you walk, and there's no such thing as "wasted time" anymore. When the sun comes out again, you wave to your oldest friend and it waves back." —Les Matheson

Life often feels like an ever-accelerating race, where we relentlessly pursue achievements, success markers, and tangible outcomes. We measure our worth by the number of tasks we complete, promotions we secure, or the likes and followers we accumulate on social media. This unending quest to associate happiness and self-worth with external accomplishments can leave us feeling adrift in a sea of dissatisfaction and restlessness.

Interestingly, I stumbled upon Les Matheson's advice on a Quora thread, and it resonated deeply with me. He imparts a wisdom that encourages us to shift our perspective and find value in embracing "zero" as a default state, while also detaching from the obsession with outcomes. Let's dive into these two tips inspired by his thought-provoking words.

Making "Zero" the Fulfillment Default

First, I want to talk about making "zero" our default emotional state. It's pretty simple. The essence of embracing "zero" as a default state lies in the liberation it offers. When you stop relying on external achievements to feel fulfilled, you free yourself from the relentless chase for validation. Where you are right now is sufficient.

It's a powerful reorientation of our perspective, one that doesn't entail surrendering our ambitions or aspirations. Rather, it's an invitation to recognize that our intrinsic worth as individuals is not solely determined by the accumulation of external accolades or accomplishments. In other words, our value as human beings extends far beyond the reach of society's measuring sticks.

For the anxious among us, the present moment is always a negative, always an absence or deficit. We feel like we have to act from a place of force or threat—do it now or else! If we see ourselves as constantly in this form of mental "debt," then we always behave reactively and from a place of fear. If you see the zero of the present moment as completely full and enough as it is, then you give yourself the ability to act from curiosity, creativity, or the desire to grow.

By embracing this perspective, we can free ourselves from the anxiety and restlessness that so often accompany the relentless pursuit of constant achievement. The pressure to consistently check off boxes and secure external validation can be overwhelming, leaving us perpetually striving for more without ever finding contentment.

To apply this concept in your own life, start by consciously acknowledging your achievements without allowing them to define your self-worth. Celebrate your successes, but remember that they are just one aspect of your life, not the entire picture. Practice mindfulness and gratitude to appreciate the simple joys and moments that often go unnoticed in the pursuit of grand accomplishments. Embracing "zero" as a default state means finding contentment in the journey, not just the destination.

Imagine the relief that comes with understanding that your worth isn't determined by the number of likes on a social media post or the title on your business card. It's a profound realization that can ease the burden of expectation and allow you to approach your goals and ambitions with a greater sense of authenticity and calm.

Can you just sit and revel in the fact that you are alive, right now, in this expansive moment?

When you no longer need external accomplishments to validate your self-worth, you're liberated to pursue your goals for the sheer joy of the journey itself. You can appreciate the learning, growth, and experience that each step brings, rather than anxiously fixating on the outcome. This newfound sense of inner peace can lead to a more balanced and fulfilling life where your happiness isn't perpetually tethered to external achievements.

Treating Outcomes as Bonuses

Next, let's explore the second tip about detaching from outcomes. When we're too fixated on results, our happiness becomes contingent on whether we succeed or fail. This constant pressure can lead to anxiety and overthinking. Les Matheson suggests a refreshing approach: Center your attention on the process itself. Instead of seeing positive results as necessities for happiness, treat them as pleasant surprises—as bonuses. This mindset shift liberates us from the weight of expectations and allows us to engage with tasks and goals in a more relaxed, resilient way.

In essence, when you detach from outcomes, you're essentially redefining the way you relate to success and happiness. Instead of tethering your well-being to specific achievements, you choose to regard positive results as delightful surprises. This shift in perspective liberates you from the relentless pressure to attain specific outcomes in order to be happy. It allows you to find joy in the process itself, fostering a healthier and more sustainable approach to your ambitions.

Embracing this shift can have a profound impact on your overall well-being. You'll find yourself less stressed and anxious because you're not constantly worrying about whether you'll reach your objectives. Instead, you're focused on the present moment, fully engaged in the process, and capable of adapting to whatever comes your way. The paradox is also that this state makes desirable outcomes all the more likely!

In the end, you'll come to realize that the path to fulfillment is as significant, if not more so, than the destination itself. The journey becomes an enriching experience, a continuous source of personal growth, and a testament to your resilience. It's not just about reaching the mountaintop; it's about relishing the climb, the view from different elevations, and the lessons learned along the way.

Chapter 29: Don't Sweat the Small Stuff

"If you treat every situation as a life and death matter, you'll die a lot of times." —Dean Smith

We've all been there, contemplating the audacious goal of living a life where every moment resembles a high-stakes game of survival. A life free from the relentless grip of anxiety over impending doom. It's almost as if Dean Smith leans in and tells us, "You know how you sometimes treat every situation like it's life or death? Well, maybe it's time for a plot twist."

In our quest for success and happiness, we often crank up the tension in our daily lives, fanning the flames of perpetual stress. But what if we recognized that we were the ones doing this? And what if we could pull off an epic script flip? What if we could give our approach to crises a makeover and find a more balanced way to deal with life's challenges?

Creating Mental Distance from Panic

Reframing life-and-death situations as opportunities for learning is a valuable approach that can profoundly shape one's perspective on challenges. It involves consciously shifting away from the instinctual response of treating situations as constant emergencies and instead fostering a mindset that seeks valuable lessons. By creating mental distance between oneself and panic, individuals can redirect their energy toward anticipating the insights that can be extracted from challenging situations. This approach encourages personal growth and development through adversity, transforming potentially overwhelming experiences into valuable learning opportunities.

As a child, I vividly recall a situation where I unknowingly applied this principle. I was about eight years old, and my family decided to embark on a camping trip deep in the woods. It was my first time camping, and I was both excited and anxious. Everything seemed like a life-and-death scenario to my young mind, from starting a campfire to setting up a tent. The unfamiliarity of the situation triggered a sense of constant emergency.

During our camping adventure, a sudden rainstorm caught us off guard. Our campsite turned into a soggy mess, and our carefully prepared food was drenched. Initially, panic set in, and I remember feeling a sense of despair. My father, however, always the wise and composed figure in such situations, offered a different perspective.

He encouraged us to view this unexpected turn of events as an opportunity to learn about adaptability and resilience. Instead of dwelling on the inconvenience, he suggested that we embrace the chance to grow and develop through this challenge. We set about finding ways to improve our campsite's drainage, creatively salvaging our wet food and adjusting our plans to accommodate the weather.

This childhood experience left a lasting impression on me. It was my first lesson in reframing a seemingly dire situation as a valuable opportunity for learning and personal development. Instead of succumbing to panic, I learned to focus on the practical lessons that could be gleaned from adversity. This early exposure to the concept has shaped my approach to challenges throughout my life, encouraging me to seek growth and knowledge even in the face of life-and-death moments. I left that camping trip with a strengthened belief in my own self-efficacy and the knowledge that I was capable of surviving, of finding creative solutions—even of laughing at myself in the midst of adversity. Looking back now, those skills seem more valuable to me than the ability to simply have things go my way.

Consulting Different Opinions

Another valuable tip to navigate such moments is to seek balanced perspectives in the face of perceived emergencies. This means actively reaching out to varied sources for opinions and viewpoints, allowing you to gain a more comprehensive understanding of the circumstances and make more informed decisions.

My childhood was interesting, but there's also a moment in my teenage years that taught me the importance of seeking balanced perspectives. I was working late into the night on a crucial school English assignment, typing away on my computer. I was almost done with my essay on Moby Dick, but my computer suddenly froze, and I hadn't saved my work. Panic set in as I realized the due date was the following morning. My initial reaction was one of sheer frustration and despair. I felt like the world was crashing down around me, and I had no idea how to recover my lost work.

In my distressed state, I decided to reach out to my older sister for help. She was always the calm and collected one in our family, the person everyone turned to in moments of crisis. She listened to my frantic account of what had happened and then suggested we consult our neighbor, Mr. Johnson, who was a computer whiz. Despite my skepticism in that moment, I agreed.

When we explained the situation to Mr. Johnson, he didn't react with the same level of panic I had been feeling. He calmly examined my computer, retrieved my lost document, and explained the importance of regular backups. His perspective was a stark contrast to my emotional turmoil. Through this experience, I learned that seeking alternative viewpoints, even in moments of perceived emergencies, can provide invaluable insights that help us regain our balance.

The overall theme of this lesson extends beyond the realm of technology mishaps. It emphasizes the importance of being present and mindful when faced with crises, and how seeking balanced perspectives can help reduce anxiety and overthinking. By consulting trusted friends, mentors, or experts who offer different viewpoints, we can gain a more objective understanding of the situation and make better decisions.

It's a wonderful thing when we have the presence of mind to shift our own perspective. But we can also achieve this shift by simply talking to people who are not currently embroiled in the drama that we are. Talking to people can instantly shed a different light on our problem, and it's also a reminder that we don't have to face emergencies alone; there are people and resources available to help us navigate through them with greater clarity and composure.

Chapter 30: Getting Comfy with the Gray Areas

"To think in terms of either pessimism or optimism oversimplifies the truth. The problem is to see reality as it is." —Thich Nhat Hạnh

In the grand symphony of life, we often find ourselves swinging between the extremes of pessimism and optimism. Like a pendulum that can't decide its direction, we grapple with the complexities of reality, searching for that elusive balance. It's as if we're standing in a room with two doors—one labeled "Pessimism" and the other "Optimism"—and we're constantly torn between which one to enter. But perhaps there's a third door, hidden in the shadows, one that reads, "Reality as it is."

Thich Nhat Hạnh reminds us that the world we inhabit is far from binary. It's not a realm of perpetual sunshine or eternal storms. Rather, it's a place where nuance and shades of gray are the norm. To navigate it with clarity and resilience, we must cultivate a balanced perspective. This entails recognizing that reality is a multifaceted gem, each facet holding a unique piece of the truth.

Beyond Pessimism and Optimism

Maintaining a balanced perspective is a fundamental aspect of navigating life's challenges and opportunities effectively. Instead of succumbing to the extremes of pessimism or blind optimism, adopting a balanced perspective allows individuals to make well-informed decisions and foster resilience. This approach acknowledges that reality is seldom black and white; it is often complex, nuanced, and filled with subtlety. By embracing this mindset, individuals can better navigate the intricacies of various situations and events.

One crucial aspect of cultivating a balanced perspective is the recognition of our own biases and automatic judgments. Humans are inherently biased, and these biases can cloud our judgment and lead us to hasty conclusions. Therefore, it is essential to engage in introspection and self-awareness, challenging our preconceived notions and prejudices. By doing so, we become better equipped to approach situations with an open mind, ready to consider different viewpoints and factors.

Incorporating a balanced perspective also involves a commitment to gathering information and seeking out diverse perspectives. In today's interconnected world, information is readily accessible, but its quality can vary widely. It's vital to be discerning consumers of information, to evaluate sources critically, and to weigh the evidence before forming conclusions. This approach not only helps us make informed decisions but also promotes intellectual growth and empathy.

Now, let me tell you about Hilary, whom I met at a writer's convention. She was a writer who epitomized the value of a balanced perspective. As a writer, she understood the importance of exploring the depth and complexity of characters and situations in her stories. She believed that real-life situations were no different. In her interactions with fellow writers and attendees at the convention, Hilary was known for her open-mindedness and willingness to listen to differing viewpoints.

One evening, during a heated panel discussion on the merits of various writing styles, Hilary found herself in the middle of a passionate debate. While some writers championed the traditional, others advocated for experimental forms. Instead of taking sides, Hilary actively engaged with both camps, asking insightful questions and seeking to understand their perspectives.

She recognized that each style had its merits and that the truth lay in the blend of tradition and innovation.

Hilary's ability to maintain a balanced perspective extended beyond writing. In her personal life, she was known for her calm and thoughtful approach to problem-solving. Her willingness to consider multiple angles, challenge her biases, and gather information made her a respected and admired figure among her peers—peers from both "sides"!

Embracing the Concept of Impermanence

Embracing impermanence and change is a profound mindset shift that can significantly impact the way we approach life. This second tip underscores the fundamental truth that reality is in a constant state of flux, and everything, including our circumstances, emotions, and relationships, is impermanent. By accepting this reality, we can navigate life with greater ease, resilience, and a sense of equanimity.

To begin, it's essential to recognize that nothing in life remains static. And it follows that it would be unrealistic for us to expect that. Our external circumstances are subject to change, whether we welcome it or not, and whether we're prepared for it or not. Careers, relationships, health, and financial situations all have their ebbs and flows. Embracing impermanence means avoiding rigid attachment to specific outcomes or situations, as this attachment can lead to suffering when change inevitably occurs.

Moreover, this concept applies to our internal world as well. Our emotions and mental states are ever-changing. Happiness, sadness, anger, and peace are fleeting experiences that come and go. By not overly identifying with our emotions, we can better manage them and avoid being overwhelmed by transient feelings.

Now, let's delve into the story of Peter, my childhood friend, who embodied the wisdom of embracing impermanence. Peter had a unique way of approaching life. He understood from a young age that change was an intrinsic part of existence. We grew up in a close-knit neighborhood, and as kids, we often played together in a small park near our homes.

One summer, our families decided to move to different cities for various reasons, and I vividly remember the day we had to say goodbye. While I was tearful and anxious about leaving our childhood memories behind, Peter seemed remarkably composed. He reminded me that life was about embracing change and that our friendship would remain in our hearts regardless of the physical distance.

Over the years, Peter's wisdom became even more evident. He pursued a career in a field that required frequent relocation, and he embraced these changes with enthusiasm. Each move was an opportunity for him to learn, grow, and adapt to new environments. He maintained friendships across the globe, never allowing geographical distance to erode the bonds he had with people.

Peter's outlook on relationships was equally inspiring. He cherished the moments he spent with loved ones, fully aware that time together was limited. His approach was to savor the present, creating beautiful memories that would last a lifetime. Even in challenging times, his ability to embrace impermanence allowed him to find meaning and joy in the ever-changing landscape of life.

In your own life, can you set aside the need to always interpret things as either positive or negative? Can you let go of the need to hurry along some changes while fearsomely resisting others? What happens when you simply become curious about the way things actually are, rather than overly attached to how you believe they are, or how you feel they should be?

Chapter 31: You Don't Have to be a Hero

"Victory breeds hatred, for the conquered is unhappy. The calm one is he who has given up both victory and defeat." —The Dhammapada

Have you ever wondered if our ceaseless pursuit of victory might be leading us down a path of unhappiness? It's as if our lives are an unending quest for triumph, propelling us forward forever, with no end in sight. We bask in the glory of our achievements and wallow in the despair of our failures, riding the emotional rollercoaster that swings between euphoria and despondency. But in the midst of this perpetual cycle of wins and losses, we often fail to recognize a profound truth: The very pursuit of victory itself can sow the seeds of discontent. The continued trap of seeing yourself as a victim is, in the end, the real chain binding you.

Now, you might be thinking, "Why on earth would victory lead to hatred?" Well, the ancient wisdom encapsulated in the words of the Dhammapada provides us with profound insights into this phenomenon. The Buddha's words remind us of a timeless truth—that our attachment to outcomes, including our blind desire for "victory," can itself become the source of our suffering.

Mastering Non-Attachment

In the pursuit of our goals and desires, we often become entangled in the web of attachment. We crave success, victory, and validation, and we attach our sense of self-worth to these outcomes. We want to master the world, other people, ourselves. We want to be in control; we want to be invulnerable winners and eternal champions. But here is where the first tip comes in: Attachment to these outcomes can lead to suffering. Instead, the advice is to practice non-attachment.

Imagine a scenario where you're deeply invested in winning a promotion at work or achieving a personal milestone like running a marathon. You're passionate and dedicated, and you put in your best effort. This is what our culture tells us is smart and admirable, right? But as the anticipation builds, so does the anxiety. You become fixated on the outcome, believing that your worth as a person is tied to it. If you succeed, you're a hero. If you fail, you're nothing. The problem was not that you set an ambitious goal or that you enjoyed the challenge. The problem was your unconscious attachment to these things, and the inability to see that they are not who you really are.

Does non-attachment mean selling all your stuff on eBay and going off to live alone under a bridge like a weird modern-day monk? Of course not—unless you want to, I guess. To practice non-attachment, you must simply start by acknowledging that your attachment to outcomes exists in the first place. It's not a character flaw; it's a common human tendency. Beware that this also applies to people who see themselves as losers or too humble to want much—they, too, have their attachments, but they are harder to see. Have you ever met anyone with a martyr complex? Think carefully about the "victory" they may have been attached to, and you'll see what I mean.

Once you're aware of the all-too-human tendency to attach, practice observing your desires and attachments without judgment. When you catch yourself anxiously fixating on a particular outcome, don't chastise yourself. The goal is not to pounce on yourself, saying, "Aha! Got you! Look how unenlightened you are, you loser!" Instead, gently bring your awareness to it. Just be with it and let it be. Say to yourself, "I notice that I'm really attached to the outcome of this situation." And when you notice yourself getting attached to the very exercise of noticing attachments, well, let that go too.

Conscious awareness is the key to transformation. By recognizing your attachments, you create a mental space that allows you to see them more objectively. You begin to understand that your desires are just that—desires—and they don't define your worth. They are like passing clouds in the vast sky of your life.

Now comes the challenging yet liberating part: consciously releasing attachments. This is where your higher, sagely self needs to step in and help you discern the right way forward. Choosing non-attachment doesn't mean giving up on your goals or dreams; it means relinquishing the tight and illusory grip you have on their outcomes. The illusion is what you're letting go of. This is important to understand—you are not abandoning attachment because it's bad for you. You're abandoning it because it's *impossible*. It will only lead to suffering in the same way as trying to hoard and "keep" your own breath or catch running water in your palm. It doesn't make sense, and it will only frustrate you.

In practicing non-attachment, you free yourself from the emotional rollercoaster of success and failure. You paradoxically become more resilient, adaptable, and at peace with whatever life throws your way. Remember, the desire for victory is natural, but the suffering that often accompanies it need not be. Victory passes; so does loss and humiliation. What you win today you lose tomorrow. . . and then you win it again. Through all this change, stay calm and awake. By observing your attachments with gentle awareness and loosening your illusory grip on them, you can walk the path of non-attachment, finding greater contentment and serenity.

Cultivating Equanimity

Enter the second tip: develop equanimity. This is about cultivating an attitude of even-mindedness and emotional balance, an approach that allows you to maintain a sense of calm and composure in both victory and defeat. The key here is to understand the impermanence of these states and to focus on that impermanence. When you do, you'll find that suddenly things matter much, much less.

Picture a time when you achieved a significant victory—an accomplishment that filled you with pride and exhilaration. You were on cloud nine, your heart pounding with happiness. But what happened next? Time moved on, and that elation gradually faded. The victory lost its luster, and you found yourself seeking the next high. This phenomenon illustrates the impermanence of even the most joyous moments in life.

Likewise, think of a moment of crushing defeat—a setback or failure that left you feeling broken and defeated. It was as if the world had crumbled beneath your feet. Yet, as time passed, you began to heal, to rebuild, and to move forward. The defeat, too, proved impermanent.

A king asked a sage to create something for him that would always remind him to be wise; something he could keep with him to remember not to take life's blessings for granted, but also not to despair in moments of adversity. The sage gifted the king a ring engraved with the words: "This too shall pass." We can call this the ring of equanimity—and its power comes from the way it acknowledges the transience of all things.

To develop equanimity, focus your attention on the transient nature of both good and bad experiences. When you fully grasp this impermanence, it's akin to standing on a mountaintop and witnessing the passing clouds. You see that both sunshine and rain are temporary, and they do not define your ultimate well-being.

The magic of equanimity lies in its power to reduce the emotional turbulence that often accompanies both victory and defeat. When you approach life with a balanced mindset, you become less anxious about outcomes, and you overthink less. You're grounded in the present, regardless of the external circumstances. Success and failure, rather than sending you on an emotional rollercoaster, become ripples on the surface of your calm inner pond.

Imagine how liberating it would be to detach your sense of self-worth from the whims of fortune, to embrace the impermanence of all things, and to cultivate equanimity in the face of life's ups and downs. By nurturing this even-mindedness, you'll find yourself living more in the moment, less tethered to the fleeting emotions of victory and defeat, and more deeply anchored in the unchanging sea of your inner peace.

Chapter 32: Understanding Your Zone of Control

"You only have control over three things in your life, the thoughts you think, the images you visualize, and the actions you take." —Jack Canfield

Think of life as a vast, unpredictable river, and you're in a small boat navigating its currents. In the pursuit of personal growth and well-being, we often find ourselves entangled in the river's currents—worrying about the swirling eddies of external circumstances, the opinions of others, and the turbulent tides of global events, all of which lie beyond our control. It's only human to look at all this swirling and desperately want to get it all to flow *your* way.

But, as Jack Canfield wisely reminds us, perhaps it's not the river we should focus on steering. Instead, we have control over just three essential elements in our lives: the thoughts we think, the images we visualize, and the actions we take. That's it. These are the oars with which we can navigate our boat through life's unpredictable waters. Now, you might not think that those three things amount to much, but if you know how to use them, they become more than enough.

Shifting Focus and Taking Proactive Actions

Let's talk about recognizing the limits of our control. Of course we understand intellectually that we are not in control of everything in the universe. And yet when we get upset that not everything goes our way, isn't this exactly what we are unconsciously expecting?

It's like understanding the limits of your garden; you can nurture the plants within it, but you can't control the weather outside it. Similarly, in life, we often fret uselessly over circumstances, people's opinions, or global events—matters beyond our garden, so to speak. To make a meaningful change, it's essential to shift your focus and identify the areas where you actually do have influence and agency, the aspects that fall within your garden.

When you've identified your sphere of control in this way, it's time to channel your energy in a purposeful way. By redirecting your focus toward what you can control, you not only ensure that you're doing the best you can with your resources and current situation, but you are also avoiding wasting those resources in a way that gets you nowhere. This principle is akin to tending to the plants in your garden instead of lamenting the unpredictable weather. If you simply sat on the porch and complained for an hour about how annoying the wind was, you actually have a double loss: At the end of the hour, nothing is changed except that the hour is gone and will never come again. Even worse, you've done nothing to actually mitigate the wind—for example, by tying your tomato plants to stakes or putting up protective barriers to protect the flowers.

This idea seems simple enough when it comes to gardening, but it's easy to miss when it comes to our own lives. How much time have you wasted worrying, complaining, or resenting a situation? How much of that time could have been used to either make useful changes or else do the work of accepting the reality and simply moving on?

Consider a person who aspires to advance their career but often finds themselves preoccupied with office politics, coworker opinions, and the company's financial stability—external factors outside their control. By shifting their focus, they begin to identify the aspects they can control, such as their skill development, networking efforts, and work ethic. They decide to direct their energy toward improving their skills, attending relevant workshops, and building a strong professional network. As a result, they become a more valuable asset to their organization and open up opportunities for career growth.

Did they manage to change anything about the office politics, their annoying coworkers, or their company's finances? Nope. But remember, that was always the case—whether they worried about this or not, they never had any control. All that's changed is now they are not wasting time pushing against a barrier that can't be moved, or having opinions about a thing that doesn't care about your opinion.

Take a look at something that's bothering you right now. Is it in your control? Take your time to think about it. If it really is not in your control, then consciously (t might take some work) pull your attention away from it and force it onto something that is in your zone of control. In the real world, it may be that an issue is partly under your control and partly not. That's okay—identify what parts are yours to change and what parts are not, and then plan your next steps accordingly.

Mental Rehearsal

Next, let's explore an underappreciated tool: the practice of mental rehearsal. It's like a daily exercise for your mind that allows you to envision yourself in positive and productive scenarios. By spending time each day visualizing yourself feeling good, completing tasks, overcoming challenges, and achieving your goals, you are essentially training your mind to stay present, reduce anxiety, and overcome the habit of overthinking.

The mind is like a theater where your thoughts and emotions play out. Mental rehearsal lets you take the director's seat in this theater, giving you control over the scenes and settings. When you actively engage in visualizing positive outcomes, you're essentially asserting authority over the script of your life. Instead of being a passive observer, you become an active participant, shaping the narrative to align with your desires—and your limitations.

Imagine an individual who experiences significant anxiety and overthinking when it comes to first dates. The thought of meeting someone new, making a good impression, and navigating the uncertainties of a budding relationship can be overwhelming. This anxiety often leads to self-doubt, excessive worrying about potential mishaps, and an inability to be fully present during the date itself.

However, once this person starts practicing mental rehearsal, they allocate a portion of their daily routine to visualize a successful first-date scenario. They imagine themselves arriving confidently, engaging in enjoyable conversation, and sharing genuine laughter with their date. By repeatedly visualizing these positive experiences, they gradually desensitize themselves to the fear associated with first dates.

As they consistently engage in mental rehearsal, their mind becomes more accustomed to positive dating scenarios. This helps reduce their anxiety and overthinking, allowing them to be more present and authentic during actual first dates. Instead of dwelling on past dating mishaps or worrying about future ones, they are better able to connect with their date in the moment.

But there's more: They can also rehearse what they'd do in the event their date *doesn't* go according to plan. In their imagination, they deliberately conjure up the worst-case scenario and then strategically imagine how they'd cope.

This is a powerful way to take back your power and remove the sting from the tail of anxiety. Imagine there's no chemistry, a language barrier, and an awkward moment when the bill comes. Imagine your date is rude to you, or that you get into an argument. Whatever it is, if you rehearse how you'd maintain composure and cope with even a difficult situation, not only will you be able to handle it should it ever happen, you'll approach every date with far more ease and relaxation knowing that your sense of confidence isn't dependent on the date outcome.

Chapter 33: Don't Suffer More than You Have To

"The resistance to the unpleasant situation is the root of suffering." —Ram Dass

What's the difference between pain and suffering?

What's the difference between messing up on Tuesday and ruminating about it for hours and hours on Wednesday after the event has already passed?

If we are alive, sooner or later we will experience pain. But if we cling to this experience, resist it, attach to it, or fight with it, we are no longer just experiencing that initial pain. We are now experiencing the pain of our *thinking about* the situation—it's this secondary reaction that we call suffering. Pain is inevitable, but suffering is optional.

Accepting Difficult Circumstances

First, acknowledgment and acceptance do not equate to passive resignation. Rather, they represent a shift in perspective and attitude toward adversity. They involve recognizing the fundamental truth of impermanence—that everything in life, both pleasant and unpleasant, is in a constant state of change. By cultivating acceptance and surrender, we reduce the resistance that fuels our suffering. This shift in mindset enables us to respond to challenges with greater clarity and peace of mind.

I vividly remember a period in my life when I faced a significant career setback. My initial response was marked by resistance—an overwhelming desire to change the circumstances, frustration over the perceived injustice, and a deep sense of disappointment. I felt as if I were wrestling with an unyielding force, which only left me mentally and emotionally drained.

However, I realized that my resistance to the situation was exacerbating my suffering. It was akin to a tugging match where the more I pulled away from the adversity, the tighter it gripped me.

With this newfound perspective, I began to embrace the concept of impermanence. I acknowledged that challenges, like all things in life, are transitory. They come and go. If I try to hold on to a transient experience, however, that's when I cause myself the most trouble. Letting go of clinging and resistance doesn't make the initial pain go away any sooner than it would have, but it does prevent you from engaging in any unnecessary suffering—and we humans are responsible for a lot of our own misery!

The shift in my attitude was subtle yet transformative. Instead of constantly battling against my adversity, I began to navigate it. I realized that acceptance did not mean complacency; it meant acknowledging the reality of the situation without judgment. It meant accepting that I had the power to choose my response to the challenge.

As I practiced acknowledgment and acceptance, the resistance that had fueled my suffering began to wane. I found myself responding to the setback with greater clarity and emotional resilience. While the situation remained unchanged, my inner landscape had transformed. I no longer viewed adversity as an insurmountable obstacle but rather as a part of life's ever-shifting terrain. I didn't exhaust myself "fighting with reality." I did what I could and let the rest go.

Is there any pain in your life right now that you are prolonging by resisting it? Is there any discomfort that you are exacerbating by trying to fight it at all costs?

Embracing Challenges for Personal Growth

In the grand narrative of life, challenges often appear as hurdles in our path, testing our resolve and resilience. Our instinctual response to these challenges can sometimes be rooted in anxiety and overthinking. However, we can always choose to embrace these challenges as opportunities to learn, adapt, and gain new insights.

A growth mindset is a state of mind where you believe that your abilities and intelligence can be developed through dedication and hard work. It's a lens through which we view challenges not as insurmountable obstacles but as steppingstones on our journey. Instead of being consumed by anxiety or overwhelmed by overthinking, a growth mindset encourages us to see these hurdles as valuable experiences that can contribute to our personal growth and well-being.

Adopting a growth mindset means actively seeking lessons and silver linings in difficult situations, even when they may not be immediately apparent. Rather than dwelling on the discomfort and anxiety that challenges may bring, we shift our focus to what we can gain from these experiences. This perspective allows us to extract valuable insights, develop resilience, and uncover hidden strengths.

One of the most pivotal moments in my life was the experience of my first breakup. It was a heart-wrenching period filled with uncertainty, sadness, and a tangle of emotions. The end of that relationship left me in a state of anxiety, where I constantly overthought every aspect of what had gone wrong and what I could have done differently.

In the initial aftermath, my instinct was to resist and avoid the pain of the breakup. I felt as though I had lost something irreplaceable, and the thought of moving forward seemed daunting. I kept thinking about who was to "blame" and replayed certain arguments in my head over and over. I didn't realize at the time that this was hurting me more than the breakup itself ever did.

It was during this time, however, that I stumbled upon the concept of a growth mindset. I began to see my first breakup not as a devastating ending but as a chance to learn and grow. Instead of dwelling on what had gone wrong, I focused on what I could gain from the experience. In fact, it was only when I stopped reflexively pushing back against it that I allowed myself to have a surprising thought: While I was sad, there was also a little relief, now that my relationship was over.

When I took a step back, I could see that part of me was not unhappy with the breakup at all, and that in many ways the fresh start was something I was grateful for. I uncovered silver linings in the form of newfound independence and the opportunity to reevaluate my goals and priorities. I could never have experienced that breakthrough until I let go of my resistance and the idea that "I hate this. I don't want this. It's not fair!"

Chapter 34: Worry Has No Function

"If you have fear of some pain or suffering, you should examine whether there is anything you can do about it. If you can, there is no need to worry about it; if you cannot do anything, then there is also no need to worry." —Dalai Lama

Our emotions are like threads intricately woven into the tapestry of our lives, creating a complex pattern of experiences. In this intricate design, one thread stands out with an undeniable presence—fear. Fear is a useful emotion when it tells us to avoid something dangerous. But what about when we fear our emotions themselves? What about when what we fear hasn't happened and will never happen?

Amidst this tapestry of emotions, Dalai Lama's timeless piece of wisdom invites us to examine our relationship with fear, including our fear of our own negative emotions. Like the ancient Stoics, the Dalai Llama recognizes that we can control some things and not others. But he has an additional point: that whether we can control them or not, there is never any need to worry about them. Either act or accept when you cannot act. Worrying adds nothing.

Become a Problem-Solver

Picture fear as a tangled knot—a knot that seems impossible to untangle. It's at this juncture that we must resist the urge to retreat or succumb, and instead, we must unravel this emotional enigma with precision and clarity. Let's not throw the whole rope away in frustration, but let's also not panic and then pull on both sides, making the knot even tighter still.

The crux of this approach lies in confronting fear head-on, refusing to let it paralyze us. Much like a skilled chess player who doesn't shy away from the opponent's advances but instead assesses the board, we must identify the *specific actions* we can take to address or mitigate the source of our fear. This is the cornerstone of the problem-solving mindset—a deliberate and calculated response to life's uncertainties.

Importantly, worry has no place here. It is utterly useless—so you can confidently set it aside.

To build a puzzle, you must have a strategy—for example, start with the corners and edges. Go step by step. Pause to see how far you've gone, and adjust as you go. Be patient. Solving life's problems is the same: You'll need a strategy, patience, and a step-by-step approach. When worry and panic are removed, you demystify the big complex problem in front of you and make way for a clear plan of action.

Developing a plan of action is akin to drawing a roadmap through the labyrinth of fear. Each step represents a deliberate move, a calculated response to your unique circumstances. If your fear stems from a looming deadline at work, your plan may include setting achievable daily goals, seeking help from colleagues, or utilizing time-management techniques. With a plan in place, you transform your fear into a challenge—a challenge that you can systematically overcome.

You become unemployed, so you pause and regroup, then put your resume together and book a meeting with a recruiter. You get an interview, but it goes poorly. That's okay. You stop and reappraise. Why did that happen? You head back to the drawing board and come up with a new, improved set of goals. While doing this your computer breaks and you can't get onto the internet. You take a deep breath, head to an internet café, and put together a contingency plan for buying a new part to fix your computer at home. That evening, you notice you're really stressed out, so you take steps to regain your composure and do something enjoyable. In the morning, you get ready to head to the computer store, but it starts to rain. That's okay. You put on a raincoat...

As you navigate your life in this way, at no point do you *need* to worry. Is it a bit annoying? Absolutely. But problems can be solved—even big, complex ones. Even ones we don't like solving or wished were never problems in the first place. Many of us say that daily problems make us stressed, but it's also accurate to say that a deficit in problem-solving skills leads to stress. Nobody likes it, but the fact is that life is full of niggles and problems and everyday hassles. We can approach our life hassles with resentment and worry. Or we can approach them neutrally and calmly. If you can solve your problems perfectly well *without* distressing yourself, why wouldn't you?

Courageous Vulnerability

Imagine vulnerability as a portal to a hidden garden within a sprawling forest. To reach this garden, one must venture through a dense thicket of uncertainty and discomfort. Similarly, embracing vulnerability requires us to step into the discomfort of revealing our true selves, shedding the layers of pretense that often shield us from the world. Just as explorers brave the untamed wilderness, we must navigate the uncharted territory of our inner selves.

In this journey, we discover that vulnerability is not a weakness, but rather a wellspring of resilience. It allows us to peel back the layers of anxiety and overthinking that often cloud our minds. By allowing ourselves to be seen, flaws and all, we open the door to genuine connections and create the space for others to do the same.

Vulnerability acts as a catalyst for personal transformation. When we confront our fears and insecurities head-on, we begin to unravel their grip on our lives. Imagine, for example, that you are the unemployed person from the previous section. You're stressed out, you're worried about the future, and you're feeling shaky about your ability to manage the situation. Basically, you're afraid.

For most people in most cultures, this kind of fear can be difficult to admit to. Perhaps this person, not wanting to appear weak or stupid to others, decides to put on a brave face and act much more confident than they really feel. Perhaps they refuse to share with others how they're really feeling, and instead project an image of doing just fine. After all, isn't it really uncomfortable and a little embarrassing to admit that you're out of your depth, you're confused, sad, hurt, afraid or just not having a good time?

Instead imagine that this person has enough courage to embrace their vulnerability rather than deny it. They swallow their pride and vanity and ask for help. Maybe they just answer honestly when people ask how they're doing. A few interesting things may happen: They may discover that they're not alone and that many others do or have felt that way; that people are ready and very willing to step in and help, but they do need to be asked; that when they're honest and vulnerable, their relationships seem to deepen, and a sense of heightened trust appears. Vulnerability, then, is something we shouldn't fear and avoid, but something we should cherish.

Chapter 35: Pet Your Stress Away

I'm pretty sure you're familiar with the magic of petting a furry dog or a purring cat. There's just an undeniable joy in that tactile connection, one that seems to whisk away worries and troubles, if only for a moment. It turns out, this simple act of animal interaction holds a secret, and it's not just about fuzzy feelings.

Recent research from Washington State University unveiled the incredible benefits of "Pet Your Stress Away" programs for college students, who got the chance to engage with cats and dogs. Not only did their moods brighten, but something remarkable happened within their bodies—a physiological transformation that brought more relaxation and balance to their lives.

Bond with Furry Friends

Here's how you can start de-stressing with the help of furry friends: Start by seeking opportunities for pet therapy or animal interactions in your community. Why not consider volunteering at your local animal shelter? These shelters are often in need of helping hands to care for and socialize with animals awaiting their forever homes. The act of volunteering not only benefits the animals but also provides you with a therapeutic dose of companionship that can work wonders for your mental state.

Alternatively, reach out to friends or family members with pets and offer to pet sit when they're away. Spending quality time with their animals can be a joyous and relaxing experience for you while allowing your loved ones to enjoy their travels with peace of mind.

And if you're seeking a more casual yet equally rewarding experience, explore the growing trend of pet cafes or sanctuaries that permit interaction with animals. These establishments offer a unique opportunity to unwind and connect with various animals, from playful kittens to serene horses, all while enjoying a cup of coffee or a serene setting.

So, why do these animal interactions hold such incredible therapeutic power? The answer lies in the way they bring us into the present moment. When we engage with animals, we immerse ourselves in a world that transcends the constant stream of thoughts, worries, and anxieties that often plague our minds. Animals don't dwell on the past or fret about the future; they live in the here and now. By connecting with them, we, too, are pulled into the present, experiencing the profound calmness that it offers.

What's more, an animal can help us access feelings of kindness, joy, and care all without speaking a word—something that can be difficult with fellow human beings. Animals have their own quiet wisdom that can be a tonic for the frazzled, over-intellectual human mind! Begin by allocating time for animal interactions, even if it's just a few minutes each day or a couple hours each week. Allow yourself to fully engage during these moments, whether it's by playing with a lively pup, quietly observing the graceful movements of a fish, or sharing a moment of stillness with a majestic bird.

Seek and Create Present Moments

Another related tip is to seek opportunities throughout your day to be fully present in the moment. In a world characterized by distraction and the incessant hum of thoughts about the past and future, this practice is a powerful antidote to anxiety and overthinking.

The world around us is brimming with sensory experiences waiting to be savored. Take a moment to notice the colors, textures, and scents in your environment. Whether it's the vibrant hues of a flower, the soothing warmth of a cup of tea, or the softness of a pet's fur, sensory exploration connects you with the richness of the present. Make it a daily habit to engage all five of your senses fully.

Nature is a source of serenity. Dedicate time each day to spend outdoors, whether it's a leisurely walk in the park or a moment of quiet contemplation in your backyard. The sights, sounds, and smells of nature have a calming and grounding effect, reminding you of the beauty and wonder of the present moment.

Your breath is a reliable anchor to the present. Throughout your day, take a few moments to focus on your breath. Feel the rise and fall of your chest, the rhythm of your inhales and exhales. When your mind begins to wander into the realm of overthinking, gently guide it back to the simplicity of your breath. This practice not only centers you but also cultivates mindfulness.

Gratitude is a powerful force for shifting your focus from what's lacking or troubling you to what's abundant and beautiful in your life. Start or end your day by writing down three things you're grateful for. These can be small moments, like a warm embrace, or larger aspects of your life, such as your health or relationships. Cultivating gratitude fosters contentment and presence.

Engage in practices like yoga, tai chi, or qigong that combine physical movement with mindfulness. These exercises encourage you to pay attention to your body, your breath, and the sensations you experience as you move. As you flow through these movements, your mind becomes attuned to the present, leaving less room for anxiety and overthinking.

Chapter 36: Plan in Reverse

Motivation often follows a familiar trajectory—it starts strong at the beginning and the end but tends to wane during the challenging middle stages. This pattern has piqued the interest of researchers, leading to a recent study conducted by experts from the Peking University HSBC Business School, the Korea University Business School, and the University of Iowa. Their study sought to uncover the impact of a strategic technique known as backward planning.

Through a meticulously designed series of five studies, these researchers delved into the efficacy of backward planning, an approach that commences with the steps just before the ultimate goal and moves backward in time. Their findings unveiled compelling insights.

While for relatively straightforward goals, the choice between forward and backward planning appeared inconsequential, the true potency of backward planning shone through when tackling intricate tasks like preparing for a comprehensive exam or managing complex projects. In such scenarios, it became evident that backward planning offered distinct advantages. Now, let's delve deeper into the techniques inspired by this study.

Start Where You Plan to End

For the first tip, let's dig deeper into the practice of backward planning. It is a powerful technique for achieving your goals by working from the end point, envisioning success, and mapping out the steps required to reach that desired outcome in a reverse fashion. This approach can significantly enhance your motivation and productivity, as it provides a clear roadmap and helps mitigate the overwhelming feelings that often accompany the middle stages of goal pursuit. By vividly visualizing your success, you create a strong emotional connection to your goal, making it more compelling and attainable.

For example, let's say your goal is to complete a challenging project at work. Instead of fixating on the numerous tasks and potential obstacles ahead, you would begin by picturing yourself presenting the finished project to your colleagues or receiving praise from your superiors. This positive mental image not only boosts your motivation but also provides a source of inspiration during the inevitable difficulties you may encounter along the way.

But now, rewind and think of the step you took just before the end point. What was it? What about the step that came just before *that*?

As you work backward from your end point, you can start to outline the key milestones and steps required to reach your goal. This process effectively breaks down your goal into manageable, actionable tasks. Returning to our work project example, you might identify the final presentation as the end point. To get there, you'd need to prepare a compelling presentation, gather relevant data, conduct research, and complete various other tasks. By structuring your plan in reverse, you create a clear and detailed roadmap to follow.

Furthermore, you ensure that you're planning a roadmap that genuinely takes you to your destination—too many of us waste time on a plan that we realize too late was not traveling in the right direction at all.

Backward planning also allows you to anticipate and address potential obstacles and challenges early in the process. You won't be surprised by these, and that means you won't be derailed by them either. When you visualize success and work backward, you can identify the critical points where difficulties might arise. This foresight enables you to proactively plan for contingencies, ensuring that you are well-prepared to overcome obstacles when they occur.

Break Down Goals into Milestones

Second, breaking down big goals into smaller, more manageable milestones is a key strategy for reducing overthinking, enhancing presence, and alleviating anxiety in the pursuit of your ambitions. When you're faced with significant objectives, it's natural to feel overwhelmed by the magnitude of the task at hand. However, by dissecting these goals into tiny, incremental steps, you can shift your focus from the overwhelming "big picture" to the achievable progress you can make in the present moment.

Overthinking often occurs when individuals fixate on the enormity of their goals, leading to a sense of paralysis or anxiety. Breaking those goals down into tiny steps effectively counteracts this tendency by creating a clear and attainable path forward. Each milestone becomes a tangible and realistic target, making it easier to maintain focus and motivation.

For example, suppose your overarching goal is to write a novel. Instead of constantly worrying about the enormity of such a task, you can break it down into smaller milestones: outlining the plot, writing a certain number of words each day, completing specific chapters, and so on. By focusing on these smaller, achievable steps, you can immerse yourself in the writing process without the burden of overthinking the entire novel.

Moreover, when you concentrate on reaching these milestones, you become more present in your actions. You're not preoccupied with the distant future or consumed by worry; instead, you're engaged in the immediate tasks that propel you toward your ultimate goal. This heightened sense of presence can significantly reduce anxiety and foster a more positive and productive mindset.

As you accomplish each tiny step, you gain a sense of accomplishment and progress, which can be highly motivating. It reinforces the idea that you are making tangible strides toward your goal, instilling a sense of confidence and purpose. This positive reinforcement further reduces the inclination to overthink, as your focus shifts from potential obstacles to the satisfaction of achieving each milestone. If you feel stuck or overwhelmed, take this as a hint that you need to break things down even further. For complex tasks, you can often get moving again by simply asking, "What's the first thing I need to do here?" Clarity often emerges once you simply get your momentum going.

Chapter 37: Put It in Black and White

A 2018 research study conducted by a team led by Joshua M. Smyth delved into the world of positive affect journaling (PAJ). Their aim was clear: to investigate whether this program, designed to help individuals manage their emotions, could effectively alleviate anxiety and improve the well-being of those grappling with medical conditions.

Daily Journaling

At first glance, keeping a journal might not seem like such a big deal. Can it really improve your mental health? Perhaps more than you think! Imagine it as your daily sanctuary, a sacred space where you can retreat from the noise and chaos of the world, if only for a brief moment. The first step is to set aside a specific time each day for this practice. It's really scheduling an appointment with yourself, carving out time for your well-being, and making a commitment to your own development.

For me, this meant waking up fifteen minutes earlier each day, before the demands of work and daily life took over. I found a quiet corner by a window, bathed in the soft morning light, where I could reflect and write without distractions. The location doesn't have to be extravagant; it merely needs to be a place where you feel at ease, a place where you can be alone with your thoughts.

As you open your journal and put pen to paper, remember this: Your journal is a safe haven for your thoughts, emotions, and concerns. It's a judgment-free zone where you can pour out your heart without fear of criticism or reproach, even from yourself. This is where the magic happens. Write freely, without constraints, and allow your thoughts to flow. There's no need for polished prose or perfect grammar; this space is exclusively for you. Keep your journal private—it's just between you and the pages.

The act of journaling is like opening a pressure valve for your mind, allowing pent-up anxieties and overthinking to dissipate. When you put your thoughts and emotions onto paper, you give them form and substance, making them less daunting. You transform abstract worries into tangible words, and in doing so, you regain a sense of control over them. Funnily enough, they often seem so much smaller and more manageable in black and white than they did swirling around your head!

In my own experience, the act of journaling became a daily ritual that helped me anchor my thoughts and emotions, making them less daunting and more manageable. It was a sanctuary where I could untangle all the day's mind knots and start to slow down my thoughts enough to process and work through them.

You can do the same. You don't need to be a "writer" or have a fancy journal or a lot of free time. Just start scribbling and see where you land up!

The Habit of Asking Yourself "Why"

Now, let's delve deeper into a specific journaling technique that involves consistently asking yourself "why" during your journaling sessions and in your daily life. It's a simple yet potent tool for unlocking insights, fostering self-awareness, and igniting personal growth.

I vividly recall the moment I began incorporating this "why" into my journaling practice. It was a typical evening, and I found myself writing about a recurring feeling of restlessness and dissatisfaction with my career. I asked myself, "Why do I feel this way?" and allowed my pen to flow freely. But I didn't accept my first answers. I had initially journaled about all the things that annoyed me at work that day—the delays, the crummy meetings, the difficult coworkers.

But I kept asking and discovered it wasn't really any of these things that was at the root of my ongoing feeling of dissatisfaction. I realized that my restlessness stemmed from a misalignment between my values and my daily work. There was something else going on, and my daily annoyances were more like a symptom of a much bigger problem. By journaling I noticed a pattern: My writing was always most negative on Sunday evenings before I headed to work, and most positive on Friday afternoons. *Why?* This single question had opened a door to a deeper understanding.

When you question the surface-level thoughts and experiences that find their way onto your journal's pages, you begin to unravel the underlying motivations and patterns that shape your life. In my own journey, I uncovered patterns of behavior that had kept me trapped in a cycle of anxiety and overthinking. By consistently asking "why," I unearthed the root causes of these patterns—deep-seated fears, ingrained beliefs, and unresolved past experiences.

I want to issue a warning, however: Anxious people and overthinkers can turn the word "why" into a weapon to hurt themselves with. Be mindful that you are not uselessly asking questions that can never actually be answered (why is life unfair?) or questions that themselves are proof of a problem, not a way out of that problem (why am I such a loser?). Instead, try understanding the "whys" behind your thoughts and actions. Why do I believe my life is unfair? What has happened recently to make me feel this hopeless? Why do I think I'm a loser?

Ultimately, the practice of asking "why" is a catalyst for positive change—but asking why alone is never enough. Ask other questions. Use your journal to springboard into action, rather than getting trapped stewing over the same idea again and again. If your journal is taking you in circles, ditch it. But if you can, try to see it as a place where you can start to have the beginnings of a real, insightful dialogue with yourself.

Chapter 38: Put a Label on It

Imagine social media as the canvas of our collective emotions. Well, it turns out there is an interesting new study that did just that, analyzing Twitter posts from thousands of users. What did they discover? When people mustered the courage to express their emotions, a fascinating transformation unfolded. If they said they felt good or bad, their tweets embarked on a journey from positive to negative and back to neutral. The real kicker? Expressing those tough, negative emotions had the most immediate impact.

They call this phenomenon "affect labeling," and while scientists had tinkered with it in labs, this study ventured into the real-world emotions that flowed on social media. The revelation is clear: Putting words to your feelings and giving them a name can be the thing that allows you to acknowledge—and then release—that same emotion.

Emotional Labeling

Imagine you're in a dense forest, and suddenly, you encounter a wild and mysterious creature. It's unlike anything you've seen before, both captivating and intimidating. You don't know whether to say hello or play dead or just start saying your prayers. Now, what if I told you that this animal is a *Koogalong* and that it's a vegetarian, harmless, and nothing to worry about? How do you feel now?

This creature is a lot like your emotions—a sometimes confusing blend of thoughts, sensations, and feelings. Some emotions can spring on us unawares and take unexpected and unfamiliar forms. When a strong emotion descends on us, we may not know how to respond, or we may immediately get caught up in blindly reacting to it, not fully sure what we're dealing with.

But when we stop and *name* things, we gain a certain power over them. The unknown can be threatening and stressful, but when we name a thing, it's no longer unknown to us, and this can instantly bring down our feelings of threat and uncertainty. Even better, knowing a thing's name means we can talk about our experience—which means we can take it out of our head and start to externalize it (perhaps we can even journal about it!).

When the forest of your mind becomes dense with the underbrush of strong emotions—perhaps frustration, anxiety, or sadness—don't panic. This is where emotional labeling comes into play. Instead of running from this emotional creature, pause and acknowledge it. Give it a name.

By assigning a specific name to your emotion, you create a small psychological distance between yourself and the emotion. This newfound objectivity enables you to observe your emotions more clearly and without judgment. From this point, you can choose how to act, and this enables your emotional regulation.

One final tip: be careful about the difference between emotions and thoughts. For example, you might ask yourself to label the emotion you're feeling. You think, "I feel like I'm a failure." But just because you started the sentence with "I feel," it doesn't mean that "I'm a failure" is a feeling. It's actually a thought (and probably not a true one!). Don't simply go with your first label. Instead, dig a little deeper. How does it *feel* to think "I'm a failure?" If you're finding it difficult to put a finger on your emotions, stick to just the basic ones: Are you sad, angry, scared, happy, surprised, or disgusted?

"Well, I think I'm sad."

Now that's progress. Try to refine that feeling even further.

"I feel that I should have passed the exam."

Can you see that this is still a thought, not an emotion?

"Okay, I feel . . . disappointed. I guess I feel a little embarrassed, too."

By knowing that your emotions are disappointment and embarrassment, you can start to process, accept, and move on from your feelings. If you simply stay feeling vaguely bad and thinking, "I'm a loser," you stay trapped in that negativity for far longer than you need to be.

Expand Your Emotional Vocabulary

Think of emotions as the colors on your palette. Emotions are not limited to happiness, sadness, anger, and fear; just like mixing primary colors, we can arrive at millions of subtly different shades. By exploring a comprehensive list of emotions and identifying the top thirty that resonate with your experiences, you enrich your emotional palette. Just as an artist experiments with various shades to create depth and nuance in their artwork, you can use this expanded emotional vocabulary to infuse depth and nuance into your inner landscape.

But here's where the real power lies: By expanding your emotional vocabulary, you enhance your emotional intelligence. Just as a linguist who knows multiple languages can communicate with a wider range of people, you can communicate with yourself and others more effectively. When you can accurately identify and express your feelings, you create a bridge to connect with others on a deeper level. It's like speaking a shared emotional language that fosters understanding and empathy.

Moreover, this expanded emotional awareness allows you to regulate your feelings more skillfully. Instead of feeling overwhelmed by a vague emotional fog, you can pinpoint what you're feeling and take appropriate action. For example, the right course of action when you feel *scared* is quite a different one from when you feel *bored*. If you confuse your boredom for fear, however, you might try to solve the problem in the wrong way and create further confusion for yourself.

As you label your emotions, be aware that there may be primary and secondary emotions. For example, you may feel apprehensive and nervous, but in response to this you feel annoyed with yourself, because you believe that feeling nervous doesn't make sense. The primary emotion is fear; the secondary one is annoyance. This is all the more reason to avoid self-judgement and to observe yourself as neutrally as possible—so that you can avoid unnecessary layers of complexity when it comes to your own feelings.

Expanding your emotional vocabulary is not about overcomplicating your life; it's about developing your emotional literacy and making your life easier. Experiment with an "emotions wheel" to get comfortable giving names to your experience—you will get better with practice!

Chapter 39: Count Your Blessings

It's no surprise that being thankful for what you have is a good idea, but what may surprise you is that there are clinical findings to support this common advice. Let's look at a study published in the *Journal of Happiness Studies* that sheds light on the effects of gratitude on our daily lives. In this study, adults were divided into two groups and asked to describe their daily well-being and stress levels over a two-week period. One group was tasked with a simple exercise: They were instructed to think about and list things each day that they were grateful for, while the other group did not partake in this exercise, and the researchers simply monitored their well-being and stress levels.

The results were nothing short of astonishing. Those who practiced daily gratitude reported feeling happier on the days they engaged in this exercise. This in itself is a remarkable revelation. The act of intentionally counting one's blessings had an immediate and noticeable impact on their overall happiness. There were no material differences to the research group during the study, but importantly, their *perception* greatly changed—by more deliberately noticing how lucky they already were, they actually began to feel more fortunate.

Practice Daily Gratitude

The essence of this first tip is straightforward: Set aside a few minutes each day to intentionally think about and reflect upon the things you are grateful for. These can range from significant moments, like the unwavering support of a dear friend during trying times, to the seemingly trivial pleasures, such as the exquisite colors of a sunset or the taste of a sumptuous meal. The key is to pause, to savor these moments, and to genuinely acknowledge their presence in your life.

Whether your blessings are big or small doesn't matter—what matters is the state of mind you enter into when you consciously entertain gratitude for their existence. When you engage in daily gratitude, you are effectively rewiring your brain's neural pathways. By focusing on the positive aspects of your life, you redirect your attention away from the stressors and anxieties that often dominate your thoughts, and onto what may have been there all along, only you didn't quite appreciate it fully. The result? A shift in your overall perspective, which spells greater well-being, greater resilience, and much less stress.

Start by dedicating a few minutes each day to this practice. Perhaps you prefer to kickstart your morning with a moment of gratitude, reflecting upon the warmth of your bed or the serenity of the dawn. Alternatively, you may find solace in nighttime contemplation, where you acknowledge the joys of the day that's passed. Incorporate your gratitude practice into your journaling, prayer, meditation, or walking habits, or simply squeeze in a moment of thanks while you're on the subway or waiting in the doctor's office.

Consider keeping a gratitude journal, where you jot down these precious moments of appreciation. Write about the people, experiences, and things you're thankful for. The act of putting pen to paper not only solidifies your gratitude but also serves as a delightful time capsule of positivity—remember the power of labeling your feelings?

One thing to bear in mind is that you are not attempting to simply compile a list, i.e., go through the motions. You are trying to summon up genuine feelings of gratitude in the moment. Consider that gratitude and anxiety cannot exist in the heart and mind at the same time. That means if you're just mindlessly listing all the same things you listed yesterday while remaining stressed, the technique won't work. Don't get complacent!

If you're really stuck and feel like you have absolutely nothing to be thankful for, then you'll have to get creative, or even add a little humor into things. "Ah, well, I'm grateful for you anyway, splinter in my foot. You remind me not to take the ability to walk with ease for granted!"

Extend Gratitude to Others

A variation on this theme is the act of expressing gratitude to others. Whether it's taking a moment to tell someone how much you appreciate them or crafting a heartfelt thank-you note, this practice holds within it the power to create a cascade of positivity, foster deeper connections, and weave threads of warmth through the tapestry of your life.

The act of expressing gratitude is like a gentle ripple on the surface of a calm pond. It begins with you, but its effects extend far beyond. When you take the time to let someone know how much you appreciate them, you're not just sharing kind words—you're nurturing the seeds of connection. It strengthens your relationships, deepening the bonds that tie you to others. It's a testament to the idea that in our fast-paced, digitally connected world, genuine human connection remains a vital cornerstone of our well-being.

But what makes expressing gratitude truly remarkable is its profound impact on your own sense of well-being. When you acknowledge the positive impact someone has had on your life, you experience a genuine surge of positivity. Your heart swells with warmth, your mood lifts, and you become more attuned to the beauty of the present moment.

By focusing on gratitude and expressing it to others, you redirect your mental energy away from rumination and worry. Instead, you center your thoughts on the positive aspects of your relationships and experiences. It's a powerful antidote to the anxieties that often stem from overanalyzing the past or fretting about the future.

Take a moment to express your appreciation to a colleague for their invaluable support, to a friend for their unwavering kindness, or to a family member for their love and understanding. Think of people who may have supported you all through life, and reach out to them to let them know how much it meant to you—it's often the help we value most that we take the most for granted! It can be as simple as a heartfelt "thank you" or a more elaborate expression of your feelings. Crafting a handwritten thank-you note can be a particularly meaningful way to express your gratitude. It's a tangible reminder of your appreciation and a gesture that can brighten someone's day.

Chapter 40: The You Behind the Thoughts

"Be the silent watcher of your thoughts and behavior. You are beneath the thinker. You are the stillness beneath the mental noise. You are the love and joy beneath the pain." —Eckhart Tolle

Take a moment and consider the nature of your own thoughts. Do you hear a ceaseless chatter, constant analysis, judgment, self-criticism? What if there was a way to step back from this mental whirlwind and find a profound sense of peace and self-understanding? The wisdom in Eckhart Tolle's words invites us to do just that, to be the silent watcher of our thoughts and behavior. But what exactly does this mean, and how can we apply it in our lives?

The essence of Tolle's insight lies in recognizing that beneath the cacophony of our thoughts, beneath the thinker that we so closely identify with, there exists an infinite stillness—an unchanging core of love and joy that transcends the fleeting pain and turmoil of our everyday experiences.

Leaves on a Stream

The first strategy is the practice of "Leaves on a Stream." This practice is about becoming a silent watcher of thoughts and becoming aware of them *as thoughts* as we watch them arise in our awareness and drift away again.

Imagine a gentle, meandering stream, and a tree dropping leaves into the water. As you peacefully contemplate the stream, you notice thoughts popping into your mind. As they do, you place each one on a passing leaf and watch as the water gently carries it away until it's gone from view.

Gracefully, and without judgment or attachment, you do this with every thought that crosses your mind.

If you think, "This is boring," then imagine the thought floating out of your head and picture placing it on a leaf in front of you. Watch it go.
If you think, "Wow, I'm really good at this meditation stuff," then do the same—onto the leaf it goes. Then it floats away.
If you think, "I don't get it. Am I doing it right? What about now?" then you guessed it: Put it onto a leaf and let it all go.

With practice, you'll start to notice how this technique strengthens your ability to recognize thoughts for what they are: mere passing phenomena. You'll become less likely to fuse with thoughts and cling to them, or else resist them. With this psychological distance, you can discover enormous calm and serenity.

Try to practice this every day—the number of minutes is not as important as what you do in those minutes. Seek out a peaceful environment where distractions are minimal. Close your eyes, take a few deep breaths, and allow your thoughts to flow freely. The key is to maintain a sense of inner stillness and clarity as you watch your thoughts pass by. You're not trying to suppress or manipulate them; you're simply acknowledging their presence and letting them flow by.

Consider a common scenario: experiencing stress and anxiety before an important presentation at work. Your mind may be awash with thoughts of self-doubt, fear of failure, and worries about what others will think. Instead of succumbing to this mental whirlwind, you decide to apply the "Leaves on a Stream" practice. You find a quiet space, close your eyes, and begin to visualize your thoughts as leaves gently drifting on the calm stream of your consciousness.

As you observe these metaphorical leaves, you refrain from harsh self-judgment. You recognize that these thoughts are . . . just thoughts. In this stillness, you gain newfound clarity and perspective. You understand that while these thoughts are something you are doing, they need not define you, nor are they permanent. This shift in perspective empowers you to approach the presentation with a calmer, more composed demeanor.

Treat Yourself as a Friend

Whether we admit it or not, we are often our harshest critics, dwelling in self-criticism and negative self-talk.

Consider for a moment that you find a dear friend who's going through a tough time. They're grappling with self-doubt, facing a challenging situation, or simply having a rough day. How would you respond to them? You'd likely offer a comforting, understanding presence. You'd extend kindness, support, and encouragement, reminding them that they're only human, and that people care about them. This is precisely the attitude we should have toward ourselves.

Instead of berating yourself for perceived shortcomings or mistakes, adopt an attitude of kindness and self-compassion. Recognize that it is entirely natural to have thoughts and emotions, both positive and negative. These thoughts do not define your worth or dictate your value.

Picture a scenario in which you've made an error at work that's left you feeling embarrassed and anxious. Your inner dialogue may be filled with self-blame and self-doubt. In this moment, step back and ask yourself, "How would I respond if a dear friend were in a similar situation?" The answer is clear—you would offer words of comfort, understanding, and encouragement.

If your friend said, "I'm such a lazy person, I'll never get anything done!" you probably wouldn't jump in and start berating them too—even if there *was* a grain of truth in what they were saying! Remember that kindness is not really about what's true or false. To illustrate, kindness may mean saying, "Well, it's true that the best of us can get a little complacent at times. But I believe in you. What's the first small step you could take?"

By shifting your mindset in this way, you begin to treat yourself with the same love and support you would extend to a close friend. Remind yourself that everyone makes mistakes, that these moments of self-doubt and criticism are part of the human experience. This compassionate approach to self-talk empowers you to break free from the cycle of negativity and cultivate a more positive and nurturing relationship with yourself.

Chapter 41: It's All Interpretation

"Peace is the result of retraining your mind to process life as it is, rather than as you think it should be. —Wayne Dyer

A stubborn mind, unyielding in its pursuit of an idealized existence, often finds itself trapped in a web of stress and disappointment. Have you ever had one of those deeply unpleasant "expectation versus reality" moments? All the advice out there told you to think positive, to dream big and go for what your heart desired . . . and now you're bitterly disappointed because nothing even remotely lived up to your lofty ideals. You can blame social media for this or point to the rise of "manifestation" ideologies and the popularity of gurus who tell their followers that as long as they dream big and believe with all their hearts, they're entitled to the grandest fantasies they can imagine.

But, reality always comes a-knocking one way or another. Your attitude will determine whether this intrusion of reality is a catastrophe—or no big deal at all. Life may not always align perfectly with your desires, and that's okay. In fact, if you want to make sure your desires have the highest chance of becoming real, then those desires need to be respectful of and congruent with reality.

Accept the Gap between Reality and Dreams

This lesson hit home during a pivotal period in my own life. I had charted an ambitious course, driven by a fervent desire to achieve a specific career milestone. Every step was carefully calculated, every expectation meticulously outlined. However, the universe had its own plans, and the path I had envisioned took me on numerous unexpected detours.

Initially, these deviations from my plan were sources of immense frustration and disappointment. It was as if life were conspiring against my aspirations. I want to say I was wise and figured everything out in time—but I didn't. I learned it, as they say, the hard way, and because I wouldn't let go of unrealistic expectations, they were basically taken from me. I had to accept this—there was no choice. But I realized that this acceptance wasn't a surrender to mediocrity or a compromise of my dreams, but a recognition of the fact that my dreams needed reappraisal.

I realized that my disappointment wasn't a punishment from the universe—it was a sign that it was *me* who was being unreasonable. I began to ask myself hard questions: What were my expectations, exactly? Were they fair and reasonable? Was I laboring under the misconception that life "should" be this or that? Was that really a fair way to think?

It dawned on me very slowly that I was stressing myself out by making demands on reality and insisting that it be something that it wasn't. I unpacked all the expectations and assumptions I had about my career and got real with myself. The truth was that I had been expecting too much of myself, and that I had genuinely believed that if I worked hard and was talented, the ride would always be easy and nobody would find fault with me . . .

I now know that a more reasonable expectation is that, even when I'm doing my best, sometimes there will be a conflict, a hard day, or a confusing turn of events—and that's okay. It turns out it's far easier to adjust your own unrealistic expectations than it is to rail against the entire universe and demand it change for you!

Chapter 42: The Value of Letting Go

"To err is human; to forgive people and yourself for poor behavior is to be sensible and realistic." — Albert Ellis

As humans, we are prone to making mistakes. We are imperfect. However, it is in the act of forgiveness, both toward others and, crucially, toward ourselves, that we find the wisdom and grace to accommodate this imperfection without it being a source of stress.

Visualizing Emotions as Balloons

Imagine your past mistakes and the wounds inflicted upon you by others are nothing more than a whimsical collection of colorful balloons, each one tethered to your wrist. Picture yourself deftly untying those strings and releasing those balloons one by one into the boundless expanse of the open sky. As they ascend, carried away by the gentle breeze, you relieve yourself of their burden.

By confronting your emotional grudges and wounds head-on and then deliberately setting them free, you become the agent of your own healing. We forgive not for the sake of others (although it's a nice thought) but for ourselves, because we may finally be ready to set down whatever we've been carrying. Forgiving others, then, is an act of self-forgiveness and an acknowledgement that you, too, are imperfect, that the past is the past, and that despite it all, you choose to move forward in lightness... just as light as those balloons that float peacefully away from you.

This liberation is akin to decluttering your mental and emotional attic, making room for fresh experiences and authentic connections based on who you are today, and not on the wounded person you might have been yesterday.

Now, cultivating empathy, understanding, and compassion toward yourself and those who share the stage in your life drama—that's a wonderful thing. When you view your own foibles and the missteps of others through the lens of understanding, it becomes easier to sever the heavy chains of judgment and resentment. But, we can forgive even if our own empathy and understanding are flawed or incomplete. We can forgive without liking what has happened and without forgoing our right to be cautious, wiser, and more discerning in the future.

We can forgive right now, today, even if we don't really feel ready to do so. We forgive not because we are "bigger people" or because we have found a way to see our wrongdoers as better than they might be. We forgive simply because we value healing, growth, and wholeness more than we value dwelling on the hurt of the past. And that's a choice we can make at any time, no matter how we feel.

Neutrality Mindset

Picture your life as a colossal quilt, a patchwork masterpiece stitched together from countless experiences and actions. Some patches radiate with the brilliance of a fireworks display, while others might resemble that time you attempted to bake a soufflé and instead burnt the house down. Now, envision each error as a solitary patch distinguishable from the entire quilt. It could be a different color or texture, but it doesn't undermine the harmonious beauty of the whole ensemble. Every patch matters. Every patch belongs. The patchwork is beautiful not because it's all one pattern, but precisely because it's a jumble of all sorts of different patterns. In the moment, a mistake can feel like everything, but try to realize that even a big mistake is just a single stitch in the grand tapestry of your life—not the entire quilt.

Try to remind yourself that a bad moment, a failed relationship, or a poor choice is not:

- Permanent,
- Pervasive,
- or Personal.

This means that a mistake is always located in time. There was a time before the mistake, and there will be a time after it. Even if there are consequences, very few mistakes are truly permanent—even burning your house down. A mistake is also limited to one aspect of your life, not *all* of your life, i.e., it's not pervasive. In other words, losing your job doesn't mean that you'll never love again or that you're out of shape or that you no longer possess any of your talents and skills. It just means that you've lost your job. Don't make a mistake mean more than it means and spread it further than it deserves to spread, i.e., make it pervasive.

Finally, don't needlessly make things personal. Did you say something you shouldn't have? Have you done something wrong, hurt someone's feelings, or made a regrettable choice? That's okay. Recognize that that's what has happened. But realize this doesn't mean that you, as a human being, are totally and completely defined by this mistake. You are not irredeemable, and doing something poorly once doesn't mean you have no choice but to do it poorly again. Doing a bad thing doesn't make you bad. It makes you a human being who has done a bad thing—that's an important distinction to make.

When you accept that errors are like plot twists in a novel rather than indictments of your character, you can focus on the here and now. The mental energy once squandered on self-flagellation can now be redirected toward genuine learning and growth—so that you don't make that mistake again. Your future self will thank you for the wisdom and resilience you've cultivated along the way.

Chapter 43: Ride It Out

"You can't stop the waves, but you can learn to surf."
—Jon Kabat-Zinn

Surfing is an artform of balance, rhythm, and connection. It's the dance between a rider and the ocean's dynamic waves—a graceful harmony of skill and nature's raw power. But beyond the sun-kissed beaches and surfboards, there's another kind of surfing—one that takes place in the vast sea of our minds. Jon Kabat-Zinn's insightful words serve as the compass for navigating the waters of our thoughts and emotions. In this mental ocean, we, too, must learn to ride the waves.

Change Is Permanent

Picture yourself on a beach, squinting toward the shimmering horizon as waves roll in, each with its own personality. Some waves are smooth and easy, others are fluffy and a little tricky to get through, and some are big and scary and hit you with way more force than you expected. Life's changes are equally varied—constantly shifting, rarely giving you a heads-up, and definitely not offering a "pause" button. But just like a seasoned surfer, we can recognize that change is an inherent part of life, the waves in the ocean.

Now, I'm not saying you should throw your hands up and let the water take you where it will. Instead, accept that circumstances will be what they are, and your only job is to be as aware and adaptable as you can. It's about learning to flow with life's changes, not trying to wrestle them into submission. Think of it this way: When you're stuck in traffic, you can scream at the cars, or you can turn on a podcast and make the most of it. You could complain about bad weather all day long, or you could shrug your shoulders and say, "I guess today will just have to be a cozy inside day" and change your plans.

To become a better change surfer, begin by acknowledging the impermanence of circumstances. By doing so, you release the death grip on anxiety and fear that often accompanies the uncertainty of change. Instead of dwelling on the inevitable problems, shift your focus to the solutions. Remember, just as a seasoned surfer reads the wave's cues and gracefully adjusts, you can navigate the twists and turns of life with your problem-solving skills intact. You can't change the wave. But you can position yourself in many different ways—stay still and let it crash into you, turn your back to it and let it carry you, or grab a surfboard and even dare to have a little *fun* with it.

The next time life serves you a big wave of change, don't be the person yelling at the ocean to stop. Be the one who grabs a board and says, "Let's dance!" Ride those waves with a dash of style, a sprinkle of adaptability, and a sense of humor—it'll make the journey all the more enjoyable.

Ride the Wave

In the world of surfing, it's not all about riding the biggest wave or reaching the shore. Surfers understand the magic is in the ride itself—the exhilarating moments when they're one with the ocean, the salty breeze in their hair, and the rhythm of the waves beneath them. It's an art of savoring the process, not just chasing the end result. This philosophy, in essence, is akin to Kabat-Zinn's wisdom. Instead of focusing solely on the destination or outcome, learn to find joy and fulfillment in the process of riding the waves.

You may be so fixated on the goal of, say, losing weight, that you start to see every meal as a box to check and every workout as just a chore you have to complete to get to where you want to be—the end part where you're at your goal weight. But living this way is like wishing away the present moment. Instead, why not savor how lucky you are to enjoy good, healthy meals in good company? Why not choose exercise that's genuinely enjoyable?

We often become so fixated on the "what's next" in life that we forget to appreciate the "what's now." Our minds race ahead, dwelling on the distant shores we hope to reach, the goals we aim to achieve, and the deadlines we must meet. It's like riding a wave but keeping your eyes shut, missing the beauty of the journey. Try to shift your perspective and recognize that the present moment is where life truly unfolds—even if it's a present that you believe is a bit boring, a bit unpleasant, or a bit confusing. These things aren't obstacles in your life path—they *are* your life path!

Think about it this way: A surfer isn't only waiting for the perfect wave but also cherishing every moment spent in the water. They love waking up and seeing what new day has dawned and what the sea has in store for them on this day that is unique and will never come again for the rest of time. There's a reason surfers can sometimes wax lyrical about their hobby—in fact many pro surfers don't see it as a hobby at all, but a way of life. Theirs is a moving, living, breathing meditation. In their constant balance and adjustment in the face of the ocean's endless flow, they find a kind of stillness and permanence inside themselves.

Similarly, you can find joy in the present, even amid life's challenges. Appreciate the learning experiences, personal growth, and opportunities for self-discovery that arise along the way. Every hardship or setback contains valuable lessons if you're willing to look. Today, right now, what is going on in your world that you are unhappy about or resisting? What waves are happening all around you, whether you like it or not? Try to see what it feels like to flow with rather than against these waves. Let's say your wave is an awful dark mood. Instead of forcing yourself to say affirmations in a mirror, what happens if you just laugh about it, acknowledge your bad mood, and "ride it out" until it passes? Just as we are impressed by a surfer who can ride a big wave, there is also beauty and skill in getting on top of big feelings... and being bigger than they are.

When you're fully immersed in the present, there's no room for the anxiety-ridden thoughts about the future or endless rumination on the past. You're too busy riding the wave, feeling the water beneath you, and responding to each moment with grace and serenity.

Chapter 44: Stop Comparing Yourself

"The reason we struggle with insecurity is because we compare our behind-the-scenes with everyone's highlight reel." —Steve Furtick

In an era dominated by social media, we can feel like our lives have to look like Hollywood blockbusters, with carefully selected scenes, curated blurbs and stories, and glossy photoshoots. With each swipe and scroll, we're inundated by highlights galore—the picturesque vacations, the radiant smiles, and the impressive achievements. It's like everyone else is starring in their own feature film, complete with a perfectly crafted trailer for public consumption.

But at this point it should be a surprise to nobody: this kind of comparison hurts our mental health in serious ways. There is a deception behind it all—we compare our boring, nitty gritty, and less-than-perfect real lives, as Steve Furtick says, with everyone else's artificially and heavily curated illusion of a perfect life. Almost always, the comparison leaves us feeling inferior—and more compelled to fake a life that isn't really ours.

Your Reality Is Bigger than a Few Pixels

The first thing to realize is that your struggle with self-worth does not stem from the fact of your natural inferiority—rather, it's a product of an unhealthy habit of comparing our entire complex, nuanced, flawed existence with a shallow, unreal version of what a human life "should be." Social media takes this normal human tendency and turbocharges it.

Instead, dare to challenge the validity of these comparisons. We must train ourselves to realize that what we are shown on social media is *not reality*—it is an edited version of what someone else wishes to convey, or what they feel they have to convey to others.

Consider the social media phenomenon, where individuals share picture-perfect moments of their lives. Imagine scrolling through your feed and coming across a friend's glamorous vacation photos in a tropical paradise. Crystal-clear waters, pristine beaches, and radiant smiles paint a seemingly flawless picture. It's natural to feel a pang of envy and question the worthiness of your own life. Yet, by taking Furtick's advice to heart, you'll begin to realize that these snapshots omit the less glamorous aspects—long flights, delayed flights, and sunburns that weren't Instagram-worthy.

Take it further and realize that this person may have gone to all the work of creating this illusion in the first place because they felt unworthy in themselves. Consider that what you are viewing is the manifestation of their insecurity. When you start to question these images rather than passively consume them, you can begin to short circuit the kneejerk responses you might have—those responses that have you feeling ugly, unlovable, boring, poor, or whatever it is.

Another example lies in the realm of career success. You may know someone whose professional achievements appear stellar, with accolades and promotions showcased prominently on their social profiles. Comparing your own career trajectory to theirs can easily lead to feelings of inadequacy. Yet, behind those achievements are the countless hours of hard work, setbacks, and self-doubt that aren't spotlighted on the highlight reel. Be discerning—you may see the professional photograph, but you cannot see the self-doubt, the work stress, the imposter syndrome, the student debt, the aches and pains, or the dark thoughts this person has at 4 a.m. when they can't get to sleep.

When you grasp this, you can shift your focus away from useless comparisons and begin appreciating *your* life. You can remind yourself of your goals, your achievements, your values, your weaknesses, your opportunities, your unique perspective, your *humanity*. You can try to remember what you were focusing on before social media forcefully snatched and redirected your attention toward something that was only ever designed to make you feel bad.

Developing Intrinsic Motivation

Step into the role of the main character of your own life. By seeking satisfaction and joy in the process of pursuing your goals rather than relying solely on external validation, you not only become the hero of your own story but also unlock the keys to staying committed and resilient in the face of life's challenges. This transformation holds the potential to make you more present, less anxious, and free from the chains of overthinking. It also allows you to be authentic and genuinely original—something in short supply in this world!

It's easy to fall into the trap of seeking validation from external sources—a desire for approval, admiration, or recognition. Sometimes, we unconsciously want others to give us "permission" to go for the things we want, or we look to those we consider better than us to tell us what our goals should even be. While it's a great thing to have a role model, remember also that nobody is responsible for your life but you.

If you've ever worried, "What will they think of me?" then you may be overvaluing other people's approval. Instead, ask what you think of you.

How would you act if you had faith in your own judgments, preferences, and desires?
What would you do differently if you knew you needed nobody's permission to do what you wanted to do?
What would you try if you were unconcerned about the judgment of other people?
What do you bring to the table that nobody else can?
Are you brave enough to know what you know, even if others don't agree with you?
Are your goals your own or do they really belong to someone else?

These questions can be tricky to answer, but if you can begin to tap into your own agency, you may discover that a lot of anxiety dissolves. Because the truth is that other people's opinions and standards only have power over us if we allow them to.

This shift in perspective transforms you into a hero who is not driven solely by external recognition but by a deep, internal connection to your goals. Your focus shifts from the future (the uncertain outcome and external validation) to the present moment, where the magic of real life is actually unfolding.

Chapter 45: You Can Tell a Different Story

"For soon the body is discarded. Then what does it feel? A useless log of wood, it lies on the ground. Then what does it know? Your worst enemy cannot harm you as much as your own thoughts, unguarded. But once mastered, no one can help you as much, not even your father or your mother." —Buddha

Do you have a memory of something someone told you once, something that you couldn't forget? Maybe it's a careless remark that lingers in your mind, a comment seared into your consciousness that you've been carrying for years. It's fascinating how a mere string of words can wield such tremendous power over our emotions. Our belief in these words can shape our entire lives, the choices we make, and how we see ourselves. We've all been there.

Perhaps this is what the Buddha meant when he explained that our own thoughts, when unguarded, can be more harmful than any external force. If someone insulted us ten years ago, we can hurt ourselves more than they ever could by simply holding on to that insult, letting it fester in us. However, the good news is that if the mind is this powerful, it can also be a formidable tool for growth, understanding, and compassion.

What if I told you that the damage inflicted upon us by these external stimuli is not inherently in their words or actions? Instead, it lies in our interpretation and response to them. Right now, in this moment, you possess the capacity to reshape how these external factors impact your inner world. If we believe the words of the Buddha, learning how to do so means we can heal ourselves more than anyone or anything else ever could—that's a big deal!

Recognizing Our Mind's Interpretations

It's not the actions or words of others that directly harm us, but rather the meaning our minds make of them. In essence, we're never at the mercy of the world's emotional rollercoaster; we're the ones manning the control panel—even if sometimes we forget that we are.

Now, let me introduce you to Tristan, a childhood friend who, at a young age, became a self-proclaimed "geek." In elementary school, while others were mastering the art of trading lunchbox snacks, Tristan was busy unraveling the mysteries of the universe. His passion for science and math made him the subject of relentless teasing, earning him the dubious honor of being called a "brain" by his classmates.

But here's where it gets interesting: Instead of letting the teasing pierce his emotional armor, Tristan realized that his classmates' jabs said more about their own insecurities than they did about him as a person. In fact, he took their taunts and decided they were compliments. He was proud to be who he was and never accepted his bullies' labels.

Tristan realized something powerful at a very young age: that we can control the narrative of our lives, even in the face of negativity. Tristan could have taken these words to heart, decided that he was defective in some way, and gone through the rest of his life believing that he was a victim, that he didn't belong, that he was marked out to be different from everyone else. Instead, Tristan realized that he had a choice to make—agree with his bullies, or just get on with the work of constructing his own narrative about who he was. The funny thing was, in time, people came to respect Tristan for precisely the things they had once mocked him for.

He didn't bully them back. He didn't argue. He didn't feel sorry for himself or allow them to make him feel inferior. He just quietly did his own thing—and when he did that, in his own way he became untouchable.

Chapter 46: How Are Your Perceptions Serving You?

"If you are distressed by anything external, the pain is not due to the thing itself, but to your estimate of it; and this you have the power to revoke at any moment." —Marcus Aurelius

Marcus Aurelius and the Buddha probably would have agreed on a few things—the above quote being proof that they both understood that life happens in the interpretation, and not in the "thing itself."

Is your perception of the world helping or hindering you? How accurate are your estimates of the world around you?
How are you distorting reality?

If you have never really considered whether your appraisals could potentially be inaccurate, there's a good chance they are!

Evaluating Your Estimations

Have you heard the saying "Don't believe everything you read"? Well, let's also remind ourselves not to "believe everything we think." Just because you think something, and just because that thought is automatic and feels like the truth, it doesn't necessarily mean it is. Have you ever encountered someone who believed something plainly false and caused themselves distress in the process? Well, entertain the fact that that person could be *you*—and the only way to find out if your estimations are accurate is to question them.

Let's say you've just received an unexpected critique at work. Initially, you may feel a surge of anger or disappointment, interpreting this feedback as a personal attack on your competence. Maybe they're out to get you, maybe they're jealous, or maybe they're just a jerk. It's unfair, you did nothing wrong, etc.

But reflect on your initial estimation of the situation. Slow down and look at all these thoughts and feelings popping up into your head. Some of them will be one hundred percent wrong, some one hundred percent right, and most will be somewhere in between. The important thing is to suspend judgment and step back to look at things more objectively.

"This isn't fair. I don't deserve it."

Challenge the validity of this estimation. Is it conceivable that the critique is a nudge to help you grow rather than a strike against your value? Is it really completely unreasonable to expect that you would get critical feedback at some point in your career? Is it really true that everyone who points out your weaknesses is always wrong? And even if the feedback is not accurate and completely unwarranted, is it really worth getting upset about?

"They must think I'm an idiot. Maybe they're fed up with me."

Again, put this thought and feeling on trial and cross-examine it. Is it really true that getting negative feedback means that people think you're an idiot? Perhaps they're just doing their jobs. Are there other possible explanations that you're not considering? Is there any evidence for this thought, or might a more moderate alternative better fit the situation?

As you muse on this, explore alternative perspectives or viewpoints. Scrutinize any biases, distortions, or irrational notions that fuel your distress. And if you're unsure and don't have any evidence either way, then be strong enough to say, "Well, I don't know," and leave a thing unresolved—you don't need to have an answer to everything.

As you gather clues and examine your thoughts from different angles, a new, more optimistic narrative emerges. You may realize that a big part of your own distress was actually coming from the convoluted story you wove around the event, and not the event itself. Shift the story, and you may be surprised to find just how quickly your feelings about it shift, too.

The Sphere of Personal Influence

Imagine finding out that your meticulously planned outdoor wedding is threatened by an impending thunderstorm. The stress of this external event is undeniable. Raindrops seem poised to ruin your special day. Remember that it's not the rain itself, however, that causes distress, but your perception of it.

Embracing the sphere of personal influence entails recognizing that you may not control the weather, but you do control your interpretation and reaction. Rather than succumbing to despair, you could choose to adapt, finding creative solutions like renting a tent or simply embracing the unexpected rain as a unique part of your wedding story. Have you ever noticed how many cultures claim that rain is actually lucky and a good omen for a wedding? Perhaps now you can guess why!

This shift in perspective can transform a potentially distressing situation into a completely different experience.

By consciously acknowledging the limits of your control over external circumstances, you free yourself from unnecessary anxiety and overthinking. This shift in mindset enables you to be fully present in the moment and concentrate on what you can influence—your thoughts, emotions, and actions—rather than agonizing over what you can't. In this way, not only do you reduce stress, but you also become more adaptable and resilient in the face of life's unpredictable events. It empowers you to take charge of your reactions and interpretations, ultimately leading to a more peaceful and less anxious existence.

The power to revoke your distress lies within you, and you can exercise it at any moment. Take a look at your life and become curious about all the stories you are fueling and feeding, all the interpretations that you are allowing, and all the perceptions that you are giving airtime to. Remember that at any moment, you can change how much power you give to them and choose a different response.

Chapter 47: Enough Is Really Enough

"If what you have seems insufficient to you, then though you possess the world, you will yet be miserable." —Seneca

Possessing the world may seem like the ultimate dream—a life adorned with riches and luxuries beyond measure. Yet, according to Seneca, even having all this would amount to nothing if you possessed it with an ungrateful and dissatisfied heart, as if the universe's bounty still somehow fell short.

Imagine someone says, "Life is hard. It would be so much better if I had ten thousand dollars more." But there is someone out there just like them who actually has those ten thousand dollars. They're not happy either, of course, saying to themselves, "Life is pretty difficult. I bet an extra one hundred thousand dollars would make a real difference to me." You guessed it: Someone else out there has that extra one hundred thousand dollars, and they're just as dissatisfied. It really does go on forever till you arrive at the world's most obscenely wealthy billionaires, those who would struggle to even spend what they have in a single human lifetime, and *they* tell themselves regularly, "Well, life is kind of tough. If only..."

Appreciating Yourself

The wisdom of Seneca's quote highlights a truth about human nature and the pursuit of happiness. Instead of constantly comparing yourself to others or thinking about what you lack, cultivate an appreciation for what you do have. Every person's journey is unique, and drawing comparisons between your own life and that of others often leads to feelings of inadequacy and discontentment. What's more, remember that you can never really get enough of what you don't actually need. Be humble, moderate your expectations, and realize that dissatisfaction is just a few steps away from anxiety and depression.

There will always be someone who appears to have more wealth, success, or happiness. The more we indulge in comparisons, the more we tend to focus on what we lack rather than appreciating the blessings and accomplishments we already possess. And just like that, we put ourselves on a rat wheel, ensuring that we can never reach some ideal end point once and for all.

Consider an example: Sarah has been on the "hedonic treadmill" for many years now. She works hard to achieve multiple pay raises and job promotions, but every time she advances, she simply ramps up her lifestyle to match and spends even more so that no matter how much she ever earns, she always has her eye on something more expensive. Two decades into her career, she is living in a beautiful house crammed full of expensive things . . . and she is unable to derive a single ounce of pleasure from any of it. What made her happy years ago seems to mean nothing to her now. In her twenties, she thought that her dream life meant two cars, nice clothes, and a few amazing vacations. She has all that now, and yet somehow it's not enough. She wants to upgrade the cars, get even nicer clothes, and go on even more vacations . . . but money's tight, she thinks. Perhaps she needs yet another promotion?

You can see the problem. Sarah's issue is not that she needs more money, more things, or more career success. What she needs is to remember the value of the things she's already achieved. She is very good at setting and achieving goals. What she's not good at is enjoying them when she gets there. One day a very old school friend reconnects with Sarah and comes to visit her in her beautiful home. "Oh my God! You are so lucky! You're living a dream life," says the friend. Sarah realizes in that moment that her sense of "enough" has become severely distorted.

In your own life, try to reflect on the things you are grateful for in your own journey, regardless of how small they may seem. Try to appreciate how far you've come. Don't take what you have for granted, even though this is the easiest thing in the world to do. This could include your health, relationships, personal achievements, or simply the beauty of the present moment. By fostering an attitude of appreciation for what you have, you'll gradually find contentment within yourself. Ultimately, Seneca's quote and this life tip remind us that true happiness is an internal state of mind, not something determined by external comparisons or possessions.

Detaching from Materialism

In a world inundated with consumerism and the constant need for more, it's easy to become trapped in the belief that material wealth equates to happiness. This mindset can lead to a perpetual state of discontentment and anxiety as we chase after the next possession or strive to keep up with societal expectations.

Detaching from material things begins with decluttering your living space. Imagine your home as a reflection of your mind. When it's cluttered with items you no longer need or use, it can create a sense of chaos and unease. By purging your space and keeping only the items that serve a purpose or genuinely bring you joy, you're not just simplifying your surroundings but also clearing mental clutter.

As you embrace minimalism and let go of your attachment to material possessions, you can shift your focus toward experiences, relationships, and personal growth. These elements provide a deeper and more lasting satisfaction compared to fleeting material acquisitions. For example, instead of obsessing over the latest gadgets, you might choose to spend quality time with loved ones, travel to new places, or invest in learning a new skill. These pursuits enrich your life and make you more present as you immerse yourself in the moment rather than constantly worrying about what you lack or what you should acquire next.

In practical terms, try to free yourself from the burdensome quest for more things and, in turn, lessen the anxiety that often accompanies such pursuits. By adopting a minimalist lifestyle, you're sending a message to yourself that happiness resides not in the accumulation of stuff but in the richness of experiences, the depth of your relationships, and your personal growth journey.

Chapter 48: Resilience Comes from Purpose

"If we possess a 'why' of life, we put up with almost any 'how.'" —Friedrich Nietzsche

What drives you? What speaks to your soul? What is your purpose?

Understanding your "why" isn't merely an exercise in self-discovery; it's a source of motivation, and clarity in moments of confusion. Understanding your purpose fuels your determination to persevere, even in the face of doubt and anxiety. In my own life, my "why" resides in the potency of words and the desire to share knowledge. It's the understanding that my words can inspire and educate others that propels me forward, even when confronted with formidable challenges.

Your "why" becomes a lighthouse expertly guiding your ship safely through turbulent seas. When you focus on your purpose, it anchors you in the midst of life's storms, imparting profound direction and unyielding motivation.

What do you care most about?
What would you choose to do if you had only one day left on this earth?
What would you be willing to die for?

Answer these questions and you may get closer to your personal set of values and motivations. For some people it will be harmonious and loving connections with their family, for others it will be the search for wisdom, and still others it will be adventure, exploration, and the thrill of the unknown. You may value independence or interdependence. You may seek out truth, or beauty may be more your thing!

The important thing is that nobody can decide what your "why" is for you. That is work you do on your own—and work you will likely have to revisit throughout your life (yes, your Big Why can change!).

Forging Your Resilience Anchor

Imagine a symbol or mantra that packs the punch of a motivational coach, reminding you of your indomitable spirit and your unrelenting drive to conquer challenges. Think of your resilience anchor as the trusty sidekick on your quest to being present and shedding the heavy cloak of anxiety and overthinking. It's your personal cheerleader, firmly rooted in the fertile soil of your purpose. For me, this anchor came in the form of a simple yet profound mantra: "Embrace the moment." It's like a gentle tap on the shoulder, nudging me to stay firmly planted in the here and now and to let go of the baggage of an uncertain future.

If your purpose revolves around saving the environment, for example, your resilience anchor could be an image of a vibrant, thriving tree. This arboreal emblem serves as a potent reminder of your commitment to Mother Earth. When life's tempests blow your way, gazing upon this image is like a sip of resilience-infused herbal tea—it rejuvenates your spirit and reinforces your determination to overcome obstacles for the greater good.

Remember, this concept isn't about mere positive thinking. It's about strapping on your resilience boots, which are made from the leather of your "why," and trekking through life's treacherous terrain with purpose. When adversity appears, your resilience anchor helps you stand firm, strengthening your belief in your own ability to rise above life's challenges.

In my own life, this anchor has been a lifeline during moments of uncertainty or when faced with the formidable foes of setbacks. It serves as my constant reminder that, regardless of how rough the seas of life become, my "why" remains unshakable. It's the secret sauce that fuels my determination to keep moving forward, to cherish each moment, and to march ahead with the clarity of purpose as my guiding star.

Chapter 49: Make Friends with Your Demons

"First, you'd discover that the monster was not real. You'd realize that it was just an illusion that you never had anything to fear in the first place. You'd see that the monster had no teeth. This would be an incredible triumph." —David D. Burns

Do you remember those childhood days when we would eagerly sit in front of the television, watching our favorite cartoons? Back then, the monsters on the screen, whether they were lurking under beds or hiding in closets, held a peculiar fascination for us. We'd watch with a mix of fear and curiosity, knowing that these imaginary creatures couldn't harm us. Fast forward to adulthood, and we find ourselves facing a different kind of monster—our own mind monsters. These are the fears, anxieties, and challenges that haunt our thoughts and can often feel just as daunting as the fictional creatures we watched on TV.

In this journey of confronting our inner monsters, we can draw inspiration from David D. Burns's thought-provoking quote, which hints that these adult mind monsters may not be as formidable as they seem. Much like the monsters in our childhood cartoons, they may turn out to have "no teeth" and be mere illusions.

Getting To Know Your "Monster"

Burns's philosophy provides a roadmap for conquering these inner monsters, and the first tip is to identify them with precision. It's like taking inventory of the creatures lurking within the labyrinth of your psyche. This process involves a conscious effort to recognize the specific fear, anxiety, or challenge that is causing you distress. It's about giving shape and form to the nebulous specters that haunt your thoughts.

Imagine, for instance, that you find yourself experiencing discomfort and anxiety in social situations. The mere thought of meeting new people or attending social events sends your heart racing and palms sweating. In this scenario, social anxiety becomes your "monster." It's that relentless fear that you might say something embarrassing, that others will scrutinize your every move, or that you'll find yourself awkwardly isolated in a crowded room.

Let me share the story of someone I know, Brad, who grappled with social anxiety for years. He often turned down invitations to gatherings, fearing the judgment of others and the prospect of stumbling through conversations. His "monster" was a shadowy presence that followed him, casting doubt and discomfort wherever he went. But then, Brad decided it was time to confront this particular demon.

Brad began the process by clearly defining his social anxiety. He named it, painted a vivid mental picture, and even gave it an amusing nickname. By personifying his fear in this way, he transformed it from an abstract, overwhelming force into something tangible—a mischievous character he could engage with. This shift in perspective marked the beginning of his journey toward understanding and ultimately taming his "monster."

By acknowledging the presence of social anxiety in his life, Brad was able to seek support and implement strategies to manage it. Gradually, he found his confidence growing, and he started to relish social interactions that were once daunting. His "monster" had lost some of its power, thanks to his willingness to confront it head-on and define it in his own terms.

In the same vein, you, too, can embark on this transformative journey of identifying your "monster." By taking the time to recognize your specific fears, anxieties, or challenges and define them clearly in your mind, you lay the foundation for empowerment and self-discovery.

Investigating Your Monster's Source

Much like a magician revealing the secrets of a trick, we can unveil the "monster's" lack of teeth by taking a closer look at the situations that trigger our fear or anxiety.

Consider, for a moment, the fear of heights—an anxiety that can cast a shadow over outdoor adventures, such as hiking trips that involve crossing bridges suspended high above rocky ravines. In this scenario, the "monster" is your fear of the bridge collapsing or some catastrophic event occurring. But before you succumb to fear's grip, let's apply Burns's principle of challenging the perceived power.

Imagine joining Lily, a person who once trembled at the thought of crossing such bridges. Armed with a newfound perspective, Lily decided to confront her fear head-on. She embarked on a hike that led her to a towering suspension bridge, a true test of her mettle. But instead of imagining disaster scenarios, she decided to become a detective of sorts.

Lily took a deep breath and examined the evidence. She observed the sturdy engineering of the bridge, noted the regular flow of hikers crossing without any issues, and reflected on the countless safe bridge crossings that occurred daily. Lily recognized that her fear had exaggerated the threat. Catastrophic bridge collapses were exceptionally rare, and the structure was designed to withstand the stresses of normal usage.

By objectively assessing the situation, Lily was able to gain a clearer understanding of the actual impact her fear held over her. She realized that her "monster" had no teeth—it was merely a shadow, a trick of the mind. With this newfound insight, she confidently stepped onto the bridge and crossed it without the paralyzing anxiety that once plagued her.

The lesson here extends beyond bridges and heights; it's a broader metaphor for life. We all have our personal bridges to cross, whether they involve career changes, challenging relationships, or facing uncertainties. When we confront these situations with a critical eye, examine the evidence, and evaluate the true likelihood of catastrophic events, we often find that our "monsters" are mere illusions.

Chapter 50: Have a Growth Mindset

Having a fixed mindset, the unwavering belief that your abilities and intelligence are etched in stone, can sometimes make life feel like a never-ending pop quiz you haven't studied for. And if you're navigating the twists and turns of life, juggling work, relationships, and the occasional existential crisis, that pop quiz feeling can easily evolve into full-blown anxiety.

In contrast, the "growth mindset" is the belief that talents aren't handed out like golden tickets but can actually be cultivated through good ol' sweat and elbow grease. Tao Weidong and their team decided to look more closely at the influence of growth mindset on mental health.

The results? Individuals who embraced a growth mindset reported significantly fewer "mental health issues" and lower levels of "stress due to life events" than their fixed mindset counterparts.

Uncovering a Setback's Lesson

One powerful strategy emerges from the heart of the growth mindset philosophy: Whenever you encounter a challenge, setback, or difficult situation, ask yourself, "What can I learn from this?" It's a deceptively simple question, but its impact is profound. This question works as a mental pivot, redirecting your focus from the daunting negative aspects of a situation toward the untapped opportunities for personal growth and improvement.

Imagine life as a journey filled with a series of doors, some leading to sunshine, while others hide challenges behind them. When you encounter a closed door, it's natural to feel frustrated, even anxious. This is where the growth mindset comes in. Instead of banging your head against that closed door, the growth mindset hands you a key with the words "What can I learn from this?" engraved on it.

So, you insert the key, turn it, and voilà, the door swings open. Inside, you find a room filled with valuable lessons and insights, like treasures waiting to be discovered. The growth mindset doesn't magically make your problems disappear, but it equips you with a lantern to navigate the darkest corners of your challenges, illuminating the path forward with newfound wisdom.

Let's say, for instance, you've encountered a professional setback at work. Your fixed mindset might lead you to ruminate on how you're not cut out for your job or how you're destined for failure. But, with the growth mindset question in hand, you approach it differently. You reflect on what led to the setback, what skills you might need to improve, and how this experience can be a steppingstone to future success. In this way, you not only reduce anxiety about the setback but also actively harness it as a catalyst for self-improvement.

Embracing the Discomfort Zone

Let me ask you something: How long have you been in your comfort zone? Well, you know, it's that cozy, well-worn space where life feels safe, predictable, and, well, comfortable. It's a place we all retreat to at times, like a haven from the storms of uncertainty and change. But what if I told you that stepping outside that comfort zone, embracing discomfort, is the key to personal growth and a path to a more present, less anxious existence?

The wisdom of this approach is beautifully encapsulated in the age-old adage "Life begins at the end of your comfort zone." It's an open invitation to take a leap off into the deep end of the pool. Initially, you may feel uneasy, your limbs awkwardly flailing as you try to swim. But with each stroke, you move farther from the safety of the shore. The initial discomfort gives way to confidence, and soon, the water becomes something to explore rather than a source of anxiety.

Similarly, personal growth thrives on exposing yourself to small doses of discomfort. If, for instance, public speaking sends shivers down your spine, start by practicing in front of a mirror or with a trusted friend. The initial unease becomes your training ground. As you gradually progress to speaking in front of larger audiences, the discomfort remains, but your confidence steadily takes center stage.

Chapter 51: Avoid Choice Paralysis

The modern world can sometimes feel like an endless giant menu. From the moment we wake up and ponder our breakfast choices to the multitude of decisions we make throughout the day, the sheer number of options can be overwhelming. It's a paradox of abundance that, while it promises more freedom, often leaves us trapped in the quagmire of choice. Researchers from Columbia University have unearthed a curious phenomenon that challenges our conventional wisdom about choice and its impact on our well-being, particularly in the context of anxiety.

According to these researchers, while we typically associate personal choice with positive outcomes, recent experimental studies have challenged this notion. These studies discovered that when individuals were presented with a limited choice of six options, as opposed to twenty-four or thirty, they were more inclined to buy gourmet jams or chocolates and complete optional class essay assignments. Moreover, participants expressed higher satisfaction with their choices and produced superior essays under conditions of limited choice. These findings indicate that an excess of choices can diminish motivation and satisfaction, shedding light on how the overwhelming abundance of options in our lives can contribute to feelings of anxiety.

Limiting Your Options

The way forward is simple: Limit your options. Instead of attempting to swim through the endless sea of choice, take the lifeguard's advice and stay within the safe bounds of six options or fewer. Not only does this make your decision-making process smoother, but it also cuts anxiety down to size.

Now, say you're in the grocery store, attempting to decipher the intricate hieroglyphics of labels on a wall of cereal boxes. Instead of getting lost in the maze of choices, draft a list of your breakfast essentials and stick to it like glue. When planning a vacation, forget about globe-trotting to every corner of the world—pick a few destinations that genuinely set your wanderlust on fire. By setting these boundaries, you're not just making life simpler; you're freeing up time to get on with the business of actually enjoying what you choose.

We may believe that more choice will make us happier, but the more choice we have, the greater the feeling that we may make the wrong one, and that the right one may be tantalizingly just around the corner. The truth is that people tend to be pretty happy with the choices they end up making, whatever they are. You may waste enormous amounts of time and stress trying to refine a choice, when that refinement does not realistically bring any extra value to your life.

For a simple example, you probably want to choose the right peanut butter at the store by deciding if you want smooth or chunky, and finding one that's mid-priced, but beyond those simple choices, there are likely only diminishing returns. If you spend twenty-five minutes poring over the labels of twenty different peanut butter brands, will any potential tiny benefits really justify that lost twenty-five minutes? Consider that the alternative was to buy either chunky or smooth without a further thought, and get on with your life. Chances are the peanut butter you chose will be just fine! The illusion that you could gain something extra by fretting the decision was just that... an illusion.

What about big life decisions? Imagine you're at a crossroads, pondering a career change that feels as daunting as scaling Mount Everest. Instead of chasing every mirage on the horizon, trim down your options to a select few that resonate with your aspirations and values. This focused approach will have you channeling your energy like a laser beam, leading to decisions that are not just good enough but uniquely suited to your journey.

When life serves up a banquet of options, don't overindulge. Just pick a few delectables, quickly, and watch your anxiety evaporate. Your path to a simpler, less anxiety-ridden life starts with embracing the art of limiting options.

Letting Go of "Perfect" Decisions

Imagine standing before a vast buffet of options, each one promising to be more delicious and satisfying than the last. The fear of making the "wrong" choice can lead to indecision, anxiety, and a missed opportunity to enjoy a meal that might have been just right. Similarly, in the pursuit of perfection, we can become so paralyzed by the fear of making a "mistake" that we hesitate to take action, stalling progress and growth.

So, decide not to let the pursuit of perfection paralyze your decision-making. Recognize that perfection is often an unattainable mirage, much like trying to explore every option on a boundless menu. Instead, aim for "good enough," a destination that allows you to move forward, make progress, and achieve your goals without being ensnared by the quicksand of overthinking.

When working on a project, for example, remember that completing it to a "good enough" standard allows you to move on to the next challenge, whereas endlessly chasing perfection can lead to stagnation and anxiety. Similarly, when setting personal goals, recognize that aiming for continuous improvement and progress is more sustainable than the unrealistic pursuit of perfection once and for all. The pursuit of perfection can ironically lead to self-doubt and the constant fear of falling short. The paradox is that being okay with good enough tends to encourage the sort of behavior that genuinely allows you to improve.

By embracing the "good enough" mentality, you acknowledge that life, like a diverse menu, offers a range of options, none of which are perfect. This insight makes it easier for you to make snap decisions without being paralyzed with the abundance of choices.

www.ingramcontent.com/pod-product-compliance
Lightning Source LLC
Chambersburg PA
CBHW060600080526
44585CB00013B/631